Creation of New India

(English translation of "Pakhand Mukt Bharat")

Pankaj K. Singh

DIAMOND BOOKS

www.diamondbook.in

© Author

Publisher : Diamond Pocket Books (P) Ltd.
X-30, Okhla Industrial Area, Phase-II
New Delhi-110020
Phone : 011-40712200
E-mail : sales@dpb.in
Website : www.diamondbook.in

Creation of New India (English translation of "Pakhand Mukt Bharat")
By : *Pankaj K. Singh*

*"Due to discriminations we became slaves,
Now let us break this discrimination."*

Author's Profile

Pankaj K. Singh is one of the leading writers of the country, who writes on suggestive subjects of national importance. His writings provide a new vision and insight to readers and general citizens to understand the subject. The books written by Pankaj K. Singh in the past 'Samarth Bharat' and 'Bhartiya Videsh Niti' have been highly appreciated by the readers throughout the country. Pankaj K. Singh has a good understanding on the topics of national importance. Due to his extensive contemplation and vivid experience, his articles, which are regularly published in national newspapers and magazines, are highly readable and factual. Pankaj K. Singh has been doing extensive research and studies on all those subjects and areas which can become the standard of establishing India as a powerful, prosperous and developed nation.

This important point has been discussed in the book, that despite many disabilities, superstitious and conservative obsolescents, that have been hunted for centuries in India, how it can be established as an egalitarian and balanced society with a qualitative-based and scientific approach.

Published books

'Samarth Bharat', 'Bhartiya Videsh Niti', 'Badlo Aadatein, Badlega Desh',
'Pakhandmukt Bharat', 'Jaisi Shiksha Waisa Desh',
'Ye Hain to Hum Hain', 'Paryavaran Bachayen Jaage aur Jagaayen',
'Swachh Bharat' (English and Hindi), We are B'coz of You (Women Empowerment)

E-mail: pkstiger@gmail.com   **Website** www.pankajksingh.com

Introduction

The non-equality and customary practices in Indian society, for centuries, have greatly damaged India as a nation. Despite being able but due to these evil custom India has been cursed continuously by handful of foreign invaders for 1500 years. Now, the time has come that India should be free from all kinds of hypocrisy. It is a matter of great surprise that as a nation, due to which many of its deficiencies have led India to suffer slavery for thousands of years, and those evils still exist in the society. No consciousness is seen anywhere for removing these defects, so that the nation will be strong and empowered. Today, in the vast India of 125 crores people, there are hardly few people, in the midst of the society, who has been resolved to empower the nation by eliminating these deficiencies over centuries, due to proper conduct and foresight.

It is a matter of thought that if we have to live as a slave for a day or if we get into any kind ill-treatment or our economic interests gets blow, then we get worried about it. We start thinking about those reasons in a very sensitive way, because of which our dignity was hurt. We use to start such efforts, without any delay, so that we can maintain our self-respect and dignity. On the contrary, when it comes to the degradation of the honor of the nation, then such farsightedness and contemplation within us gets extinct.

Even after the tortured slavery by the foreign invaders for 1500 years, if within this country people does not have any discomfort due to which the country was enslaved to a handful of foreign invaders, those flaws from the society, and from the nation without delay, till then nation building will be a day dream. Needless to say today's need that the entire society should be united. Every Indian citizen should consider the other Indian citizen as his family. On the basis of this kind of brotherhood and emotional relationship, the creation of an organized society and a strong nation can only be possible.

Every person in the country knows the misdeeds due to which this nation had been slave for thousands of years, these flaws are—the discrimination prevailing in the society, casteism and behavioral hypocrisy. This is the defect that has never allowed India to unite in the form of a nation and as a society. It is a matter of great surprise that even after experiencing so many harsh experiences and horrific consequences, why is there no sense of awareness, farsightedness and determination within us for the society and nation? Although some people can say that the country has progressed in this direction and people are becoming conscious and trying best for the nation, but the truth is that this process is still very slow. Most of the citizens of the country are still unaware of their duties towards national problems and social evils.

It is clear that if India is to emerge as a strong and capable nation, then it will have to utilize the huge human resources available in the country. Eligible individuals have to be engaged in the task of building the nation. It is necessary that a qualitative system should be created in the country, in which an opportunity for any citizen of the country should be readily available on the basis of merit and talent.

On the basis of birth only, if an ineligible person leverages the facilities then this type irrelevant system should be terminated immediately. For this, necessary legal provisions should be made. It is necessary that the modern India should rise above the unscientific caste system and to adopt an justified system based on merit, in which every citizen of the country can be happy to contribute to the development of the country, with enthusiasm on the basis of its capacity and ability, as it is evident in most developed nations of Europe and America, who have established themselves as a superpower and a prosperous nation by adopting an eligibility based system.

Our ancient thinkers and nationalist thinkers have, from time to time, started a comprehensive and intensive social campaign for the liberation of hypocrisy and evil customs in the society. Gradually, the country and society have started getting the best result of these social campaigns and community efforts. Today it is necessary that in every home of India there should be a discussion about nation amongst family members every day. Every Indian citizen should have high concern towards national problems.

Every citizen should have high zeal, courage and desire to work for the unity of the nation. As long as this feeling will not come up in every person, it will not be possible to build a strong and glorious India. There is a need for final war against discrimination and hypocrisy in the society. Now this war should end only, when the Indian society is completely free from caste based hypocrisy and discrimination.

– Pankaj K. Singh
Author
Mobile 09560754364
E-mail pkstiger@gmail.com
Website www.pankajksingh.com

Preface

It is very astonishing that in a country where millions of patriots had sacrificed their lives, their wealth and all their livelihood for its freedom, then after Independence from where such 'bacteria' and 'virus' had entered in India that within a decade of achieving independence, our Indian politics and social life were completely misguided and ruined.

This proved that though we have attained independence, but we could not understand our pride, responsibility and actual goal as a nation. Were we really not qualified for 'self-governance'? Even today, are we not so matured and responsible that we can govern our country in better way. This situation has persisted for many decades. Many nations like Israel and China, who got independence later on or with us only, today they have gone far beyond in every field of life. As a nation, India and 125 crores citizens living here, should think over on this. It will not be easy to replenish it. The time India should have utilized for building its infrastructure and in the mental development and character building of its citizens, that precious time India has already lost.

Even today, many social evils and hypocrisy are spread across the country. To get rid of it, the whole country needs to be united and stand against it. There is a need to eradicate all types of vested interests and characteristic weaknesses from Indian social and political life. Whenever there is a bias on the narrow grounds of caste, religion, region and language in the country, it always leads to disqualification and chaos. With this, the morale of qualified and talented individuals get weak. It is clear that by breaking the morale of their hard-working, meritorious and capable citizens, a nation can never move forward.

Whenever there is an expectation of loss of religion and nation, then the war becomes inevitable. Although every efforts should be made to combat the war, but there is a limit. Treaty cannot be done by keeping the self-esteem of the nation on hold. Indian nationals should always be ready for all types of sacrifices for the revival of the nation and society. It has also been clarified in the Mahabharata's 'Strenuousness Festival' that all efforts of peace should be tried before war. Hindu, Muslim, Sikh, Christian or any other religious person being a citizen of this country cannot separate themselves from the national boundaries. It should be noted that any work, which is anti-national, can never be 'Religious'.

Today, most of the problems have been generated in the country only because the average Indians have become slaves of 'economic benefits' and 'greed'. It requires serious contemplation and churning on how and when such characteristic weakness has entered the country? Why have we become so accustomed to extreme security on this land of renunciation and sacrifice? Today we are living a life like this, as if we have conquered 'Time' and we have become immortal for an eternity.

By giving priority to materialistic objects our whole life and attention has been confined in the collection of these objects. Apart from this, as if there is no such goal of life. How can things and different types of consumer products finally become an alternative to high values of contemplation, high values of philosophy and national consciousness? Can a person's life and his goal be limited to just raising and earning a living? Not at all.

Most Indian citizens today are victims of indiscipline. Due to this indiscipline, we are not able to achieve the expected success in every field. The country has to suffer the consequences of in-activism and indiscipline. Why can't we be happy in national interest? Looking at the problems of the country, as a citizen, why should we not sincerely discharge our responsibility?

In this book, the important point which has been discussed is, for centuries, India, being victim of many inequalities, superstitious and sophisticated innocence, can be established as an egalitarian and balanced society with a qualitatively-based and scientific approach. The writer has successfully attracted the attention of nation's citizens to the very important issues through suggestive facts, fluent writings and interesting language. A must read book for every one.

– Indresh Kumar
(Eminent Thinker & Ideologue)

Contents

1

Education without
National Consciousness

The construction of any civilization and human society essentially hinges upon the richness and self-esteem of their education system and the language culture. Today, the need for a change in Indian education system and educational courses is being felt. In fact, this demand has been going on for several decades. In the liberated India, the education system and educational courses that required to be infused with the spirit of nation building has not been done so far. Due to long-term dependence of foreign invaders and for a long period of colonial rule many types of attachments, connotations and inferiority complex had penetrated in the country and society, the responsibility of its abolition was doubtless on the shoulders of Indian education system. Unfortunately, the first government of independent India had opted out of this liability. Indian politics with the hypnotism of colonial rule has been continuously diverted with the vital responsibility of nation formation. In independent India, the same system of education and educational system continued, which had previously became the medium of fulfilment of the interests of colonial rule.

The so-called secularist and leftist intellectuals and historians have deliberately worked for the separation of India's ancient culture and the spirit of national consciousness from Indian education system. In the last six decades of Independent India, whatever history books have been taught in the curriculum of Indian schools are related to the 'figurative' and 'exaggerated' things about India's so-called 'Ganga-Jamuni' culture and 'Hindu-Muslim unity'. In our academic textbooks devoid of national consciousness and values, the honor and dignity of the Mughal emperors has been rendered respectfully with great enthusiasm. On the contrary, there would hardly be a student, who know that during the Chandragupta Maurya period, the city of Patliputra was such a huge city that in reference to it, Greek Ambassador Megasthenes wrote that "this is the world's most advanced and vast city." Similarly, our new generation and students have very limited knowledge about Aryabhatta, Harshavardhana, Kanishka and Samudragupta. In history books, under a thought-provoking strategy, the role of revolutionaries and nationalists in the movement of freedom struggle of India has been introduced to a very low level.

In India, the history books are mostly written by those writers and historians, who have been slaves of the colonial mindset for a long time. In reality, these historians have not had any kind of quivering and intimate feelings towards Indian consciousness and national pride. Does in our history such examples of national consciousness should not be discussed more broadly, which could pulsate future generations towards the nation? Why are our history books being so miser in saying about Indian Ayurveda, Yoga, Indian Games and Indian Fine Arts, Drama, Culture and Literature, and National Achievements in this field? For any nation, history is such a trustful thing, by just remembering only the nation's consciousness takes a new look. In fact, a nation is molded in the same form and color, as the pattern and thinking of the new generation which is growing in that nation. It is necessary that the reconstruction and re-writing of Indian education and history should be done as soon as possible and it should be equipped with the essential values for nation's building.

This contaminated education system, developed by Macaulay and unleashed unknowingly and without any farsightedness by the governments of Independent India, unfortunately it was considered to be the only source of livelihood and employment generation and has actually rendered our mind towards unconsciousness. The country's psyche is actually lying semi-conscious since very long. In our education system, there is no sense of consciousness and vibrancy towards society and nation. This is the reason that most of the citizens today do not see themselves connected with the nation. If he had a slightest sense of dedication towards the nation, would he be involved in anti-national activities? All the developed nations of the world have been able to unite their citizens due to their nationalist education system and educational values. Due to education based on nationalist values, the citizens of developed nations feel responsibility and sensitivity towards their nations.

There are also some people in India who have considered the society and the nation differently. Some people have considered caste and religion as the dominant ones. For such people, the 'nation' has become a secondary topic. Indeed, such separated and isolated thinking is only due to ignorance and lack of farsightedness. Such narrow thinking can never take us, our society and nation anywhere. By this narrow thinking neither of the individual nor of his caste and creed nor will there be any kind of welfare of the nation and society in a broad and comprehensive manner. We must keep in mind that as long as the country is competent, independent and strategically safe, until then we can also keep ourselves safe and independent. Without the interests of the society and the nation, individually as a citizen there is as such no benefit can be possible.

Today, there is a great need for connecting school children directly with important issues of the nation. If as a student these children become aware of national problems and become reflective of their resolve, then certainly a better nation can be built. Every year dates of national importance, national and international days associated with environment and energy conservation should be celebrated as festivals in schools. With this, Indian students will continue to realize their responsibilities and going to remember their obligations towards the nation. It is the practice of celebrating all the important dates in a very enthusiastic and creative manner, declared by the United Nations, in developed countries related to national heroes. Such types of creative habits should also be developed in Indian schools and society. This creativity not only connects entire citizens to a thread, but also increases the national pride.

Due to long-term slavery and colonial rule, there has always been a perception in India that Indian education system has been manipulated by the foreign invaders on a large scale and there has been conspiracy to make Indian education worthless in a planned manner. The feeling of 'nationalism' in Indian citizens due to valueless education could not be predominant. Indian education does not connect the new generation with the great emotion of national ideas and nationalism. In fact, while emphasizing this assumption, we should also keep in mind that whether India has been so weak and poor as a society and a nation that only a handful of foreign invaders continued to attack Indian education and society and continued to rob it uninterruptedly.

As a vast nation like India, it is not the right way to say that handful of foreign invaders have conspired against our country and enslaved it financially, ideologically, academically and strategically for almost 1500 years. In fact, in the form of a society and nation, we must essentially contemplate the stereotypes and problems that have existed in India, due to which a vast nation like India had to work for a long period under a handful of foreign invaders.

Since the ancient times only great thinker, intellectual, philosopher and academician have been working in India and giving important suggestions to society and system. If their suggestions were followed uprightly, then surely today India's condition would have not been so miserable at the ideological level. Some time back, India used to offer new philosophy and research to the world,

                    Creation of New India

but today it has gone below the standard of prescribed education at the international level. In the 'World Educational Index', India has reached 147th place in the world today. Whereas a small countries such as Finland, Denmark and New Zealand, they have established themselves in the field of education, at the position of first, second and third place respectively. The falling level of education affects entire society and the nation. When the education system is weak and irrelevant, it affects citizens on their ideological & psychological level.

Although many efforts have been made to improve the education system in India, but these are proved to be insufficient. After the Right to Education Act, basic infrastructure has been developed in the primary schools of the country, but the quality in Indian education still remains at the alarming level. At the primary education level in 2014, the student and teacher ratio in India has increased to 49.3 percent more than the previous years. Availability of drinking water in schools is 75.6 percent, good condition female toilet is 55.7 percent, computer availability is 19.6 percent and library availability is 78.1 percent. The level of quality of primary education is that still in India, 25 percent of the eighth grade students cannot read the lessons of other classes. In the same way, only 25.3 percent of the students till the third grade can subtract up to two digits. According to the statistics, only 25 percent of children in fifth class can read general English.

Statistics show that only one out of the nine students studying in school is able to enter college. The ratio of students who register for higher education in India is only 11 percent, and that is lowest in the world. In America, this ratio is 83 percent. In order to reach this ratio to the target of 15 percent, India will have to invest a huge amount of Rs 3 lakh crore, whereas in the 11th Plan, only 70,000 crore rupees have been provided for it. According to research by 'Nasscom and McKinsey', one of the 10 in the Humanities and one out of four engineering degree holders have been qualified to get a job. These figures are clearly challenging to the claim that India is having world's largest technical and scientific manpower.

The research of 'National Assessment and Accreditation Council' shows that the level of education is extremely poor in 90% of colleges and 70% of the universities in India and it is not conducive to standards. Even the educational institutions like IIT Mumbai, have not been able to place themselves in the list of the best institutions declared at global level. The shortage of teachers in Indian educational institutions is very high. Even among prestigious institutions like IIT, there is a shortage of 15 to 25 percent of teachers. On an average the Indian universities change their curriculum in every 10 years, but still they are not able to even touch the world class standards.

In the first 50 years of independence in India, only 44 private institutes were granted Deemed University status, whereas in the last 16 years, 69 more private universities have been given the recognition of Deemed University. Due to lack of good education institutions, 'cut off' percentage rises to an abnormal extent to get admission in good and reputed colleges. According to some research studies, the tendency of suicides among students is increasing rapidly in the country due to the pressure of scoring good marks in secondary school. Indian students spend around $ 7 billion or almost around 43 thousand crore every year to study in foreign universities. The rising race of Indian students towards foreign universities clearly indicates that the level of education in Indian universities has gone very low and it does not meet the world-class standards.

Sam Pitroda, head of the Knowledge Commission in India also says that, "Nowadays the power of governing the global economy, development, wealth generation and operative power of prosperity can only be said to the education." The basic problem of Indian education is the lack of quality. It is a bitter truth that there is no level of academic activity in more than half of the primary schools

Creation of New India

of India. The level of knowledge of teachers teaching in primary schools is also very low. Now it is time to forget about the primitive era of chalk and blackboard, and required to use the innovative world-class technology for primary education in villages also.

At present, a number of serious reforms are needed to be made at the higher education level in India. Existing higher education level in India cannot be considered satisfactory. If India has to establish itself as a superpower in the field of education and research, then it will not be fair to make any kind of agreement in the level of quality of education. The country needs to move forward with a new vision and thinking towards education reform. Now, the country needs to look far beyond the institutions such as the University Grants Commission. The University Grants Commission, which was set up six decades ago, also needs to make it compatible with the new international standards.

Today, education sector has become a huge business in India. The rich section of India is entering in the field of education for large-scale black money investments. Thousands of private colleges are being built every year in the country. Most of these private institutions have nothing to do with the education level. Almost every rich section of the country is building private institutions with high-rise buildings to increase their glory and earnings. Due to corruption, they also get permission easily to build technical and management institute. The level of education in most of the private institutions is so worst that the youth who have passed out from these institutions fail to get employment and career at the desired level.

Investment on education, provide many benefits

The task of building a nation actually starts from school itself. Our school is the largest manufacturing unit of building a nation. The educated and disciplined citizens of the schools, which are prepared in these schools, are the foundation stone of nation building. Schools can only make Indian society and nation to adapt various innovative and scientific thoughts. Enlightened students coming out of schools have the capability to eliminate all types of prejudices for national interest. It is only in the schools of that nation to fulfill the strength of nation's various social, economic and psychological needs. Many decades ago, Martin Luther King had expressed his dream in these words: 'One such day will come when a black kid, holding hands with the white kid will sit in the same bus, in the same school, and will sit under the same roof of school.'

Like America, in India also non-equality and untouchability have been a major social problem. The elimination of apartheid or untouchability or caste system can only be through the propagation of education and scientific approach. Years ago Mahatma Gandhi had said about the importance of education that it is the only ray of hope; education should reach to every person of India. The concept of the same school system in independent India was that whether the child is from any caste or religion, poor or has come from a rich family, when in the school all of them will learn and play together, then a responsible society and a strong nation will be created based on parity and equality. In fact, the path of world peace also goes through similar value based education given in schools.

Unfortunately, the situation of government schools in independent India has not been very good. Despite government figures and claims, the reputation of these government schools has not been able to save even by the help of World Bank and UNESCO. Gandhi ji said about the person standing at the end of the last line of democracy that the goal of good governance is the person standing at the end of the last line and everyone should take care of him. Their children either do not attend school or leave school after a few years and fall in to the category of illiterates. In India, billions of children use to go to school, but only to have Mid Day Meal.

Primary education in India has been divided between rich and poor. On one hand, there are wonderful, huge and well-structured

                                    Creation of New India

schools with expensive fees in the country, while on the other hand there is acute shortage of infrastructure and basic requirements for the billions of poor children to sit and read in primary schools. There is neither proper arrangement of light in these schools nor arrangement of proper sitting for children. Often, there is not even the proper path to go to these schools. Teachers teaching in government schools neither take enough interest in teaching children nor their own level of education is high enough.

Even though the government has been strict, still most of the teachers are not ready to come to school on time. In many states, in the past years, it was noticed that the teachers even did not attend school and send another unemployed youth in their place to teach. It has also been observed that teachers of Indian primary schools are largely involved in contractual and other activities and they are doing this government job only to have their pride and show off in the society. Many teachers are irresponsible to such an extent that they keep giving their personal work being done by children even during school hours. Overall, the condition of primary education in India cannot be said satisfactory. Only literate citizens, by any means, cannot be the target and base of education system of the country. The objective of primary education in India should be to create a suitable and skilled citizen.

Since 1960, UNESCO had set a goal of 100% primary education, but even today, after five decades have passed, the situation is that even today 60 million children don't reach schools. It will now try to achieve 100% primary education goal by the year 2030. In India, the goal of 69% primary education was achieved in 1999. In the next 10 years, it has become 97%, but there is still much work has to be done. The international experience clearly indicates that spending on education for the developing countries is the best investment. Investments in education are the very far-reaching benefits for developing countries like India.

Education is such element that India can be free from the vicious cycle of poverty, unemployment, inequality and insecurity. That is why it is said that spending on primary education is the most profitable deal. There is also the possibility of getting the best results from girls' education. Education is the path that can make India reaching the goal of establishing as a powerful nation.

Better education, better society

There is a need to improve primary education in India. Without this, neither the level of higher education can be improved in the country nor can efficient human resources be created. Unfortunately, the situation of primary education in India is not said to be better. The plight of primary schools run by the Basic Education Council throughout the country often keeps getting heard. There is a lot to be done to improve these primary schools. Adequate resources and administrative will power is very much required to improve primary education.

Significant efforts are going on in some states in the direction of improving at the level of primary education. In this context, the example of Uttar Pradesh can be taken, where in Hardoi district this measure has taken up. Under this, there is a plan at the district level, from which basic education officer to block education officer, block coordinator, choose some schools and teachers. These teachers give two hours of extra time in the evening to teach children from class fifth to eighth in selected schools in poor, backward and highly populated areas.

Petromax etc. has been arranged at the public education centres. The purpose of this scheme is that the teachers and schools that are selected in the beginning can be presented as 'ideal' in front of others. If the result of this scheme comes as expected, then it can certainly be an example for all.

It is worth noting that the resources available to us in the Council schools are not being fully utilized. Several schemes of incentives

Creation of New India

have been made by the government from time to time, but their ground implementation is not as concrete as it must be. There is an acute shortage of teachers in the field of primary education as per teacher-student ratio, but it is also true that even those teachers who are available are not being properly utilized. The presence of teachers in the remote areas remains negligible. Even those who are present, most of them do not teach with full interest. As far as the students are concerned, maintaining their presence throughout the school time is a big challenge for teachers.

To fulfill the attendance of students at the time of the examination, teachers have to go house to house and request not only to students but also to their parents. Several welfare schemes like mid-day meal scheme, free books and distribution of free school uniform are going on, but these measures of encouragement also have not been fully implemented. Very often, a lot of complaints of corruption and flaws in the implementation of these schemes, usually come.

In India, the number of youth are less interested to pursue careers in the education sector. They keep interest in becoming engineer, doctor and officer. Youth is not very much interested to be a teacher, therefore number of teachers are decreasing day by day in India. It is clear that when the country does not get good teachers, then how will the state of primary education, which is already dysfunctional, finally improve? In the education sector, there is a wide need for extensive research in the country today. In order to encourage youth, there is a need to make education career more attractive and honorable.

Education sector in India is becoming a big business. There is a flood of such schools in the country which are selling only degrees. They have nothing to do with the quality of education and research. These schools, which are established by investing black money, are not really going to contribute any intellectual benefit to the country. There are very few educational institutes in the country whose reputation and recognition are of international standards.

A lot of social, economical and professional problems are coming up due to such anti-national and malignant mentality of selling and buying of 'Degrees'. If the level of higher education is not improving in India, is only due to the thinking behind changing educational sector to industry is playing a key role.

With the deterioration of higher education, the level of primary and middle level education, in the country, is also not improving. Except some of the prestigious private schools, the number of such private schools has increased rapidly, with the support of few Education Department officials. They are running against the parameters, or teaching without recognition. Ironically, the corporation schools have already lost its relevance in terms of education and security. Instead of education, it has become merely a literary center.

After attaining the responsibility of providing school building and school uniform, the role of principals has now become as a contractor rather than a teacher. The role of other school staff has been limited to arranging mid-day meal and its distribution. The situation of security is so bad that the news of falling sick of children by consuming poisonous jatropha seeds during play hours or taking Mid-day meal is very common.

This is the misfortune part of India that parents here sending their children in a large number to schools so that at least they could get lunch. At the level of policy formation, it is India's irony and dilemma that either it assesses the relevance and efficiency of the schemes or thinks about the welfare of the people on the basis of their poor nutrition and humanity. A country like India has to ride on both boats simultaneously. This is the bitter truth of India's planning of independent India so far. This is the reason why, neither we have accomplished our planned goals nor has it been possible to assess the deliberation and liability fixation of the reasons responsible for not fulfilling the goal here. It has often been observe that private schools, charging heavy tuition fees, are also not adopting any

                                          Creation of New India

serious attitude towards the rising level of education for children. For them, the child has just become a consumer. It is ridiculous that private schools which are charging huge fees use to conduct a long admission procedure before enrolling a child. Not only to this, the school collects all the details of the child's family, its socio-economic status, and then conduct the parents interview too. They should be asked that if they'll get all the best and everything 'readymade', then what will actually be their role? The attitude of these schools is often anti-national, when they do not allow the poor students to enter their school. By adopting one or the other method they skip and don't follow orders of the government, in which they have to enroll the prescribed number of poor students in their schools. Due to their staunch love for English language and being the carrier of Macaulay's mental slavery are often seen as ridiculing other Indian languages. Overall, this private school is stuck in the ego of power and money. These schools do not face any problem, because those who run these schools use to have good approach in the corridors of political power. As long as the Government is not going to take full responsibility and priority the education of young kids, on its own, by then, the idea of major changes in the situation is not possible.

There has been confusion over education for a long time in India. Like in other areas, education in India is also struggling with the untimely conflict of less resources versus quality. In India a large number of children are born unplanned, and any kind of planning related to their education are not preplanned at their parents family, society and nation level. For so long, just to fulfil the target of govt. statistics and to show all the figures related to primary education, making useless plannings and efforts to complete all this, by any means.

India is such an unfortunate nation, where no serious attention is given to the future of the society and the nation. More than 60 percent of the population in India is cursed to live a resourceless life. No attention is given to the primary education of children and for their better upbringing by this vast population.

Billions of children of the country are born in unplanned manner and grow up in a chaotic manner. Such children neither get proper care and food, nor better education and enough opportunity in sports. Somehow they grow up in between the harsh truths and tortures of life. Due to lack of proper care, these crores of Indian children are trapped in bad society, intoxication and crime at a very young age. It is clear that those children on which Indian society and nation have neither paid adequate attention nor have made the desired investment, naturally when they grow up, how can they become an ideal citizen of the country? Indian primary education today has become a mere source of getting 'Lunch' (Mid-day meal). Parents use to send their children to school only because this will help them from getting away of the responsibility of providing food for their children. According to official figures, 42 percent of children leave school before 8th class, in India. Similarly, 51 percent of Dalit children and 58 percent of tribal and minority children leave school before 8th class. 64 percent of girls leave school before 8th class, in India. This clearly shows the level of seriousness of imparting primary education in India.

Contrary to India, in developed countries, there is a lot of focus and care on primary education of children and their upbringing. From their childhood only, their talent is recognized and they start working to sharpen that. At a young age only, children are given high level training in the field of their interest. These children who are physically and mentally fit, and well-educated and trained use to earn great achievements for the nation in the coming time. Developed countries have become rich, powerful and capable enough due to its excellent primary education policy and system, and better parenting and upbringing of children.

O

　　　　　　　　　　　　　Creation of New India

2

Distorted Historiography

A strange problem in India's context is that the available history in the country has been originally written by the foreign historians. In this history writing, basically the research and study materials made during the colonial rule have been formed. It has often been seen that history writing suffers from various types of prejudices. Historians in all the countries of the world have not been freed from their prejudices and love for the country. This is the reason why writing neutral history in the entire global world has been very short. In the context of ancient civilizations like India, different historians and scholars have written history in their own way. There is so much contradiction between them that the true facts cannot be ascertained. The general citizen makes misconceptions from this kind of diverse and often distorted history writing.

It is an experience that whenever any of their faults are not resolved by any society or civilization, by applying its assessment in a neutral way, until then, it cannot secure a strong position in society and civilization history. Keeping a whimsical sense of appreciation or inferiority towards history, both affect that country and society seriously. It should also be interpreted in the qualitative fact that in the form of a society and a nation, why huge India continued to be defeated in the hands of a handful of foreign invaders, and has long been subjected to long-suffering. Of course, due to the flaws and hypocrisies prevailing in Indian society, foreign invaders have been successful in defeating India. Indian students should be told about what were those faults, hypocrisy and selfishness, whose fierce cost and adverse consequences were paid by the whole nation for thousands of years. Without knowing and understanding them, how will the new generation of India be alert and free from those shackles of defects and hypocrisy? It is certain that Indian society should accept its causes, otherwise it will not be possible to deal with them as well. For treating any disease, it is necessary that first of all proper diagnosis should be done, and also for the patient to accept the disease and should be mentally and physically prepared to follow all the guidelines and consume all the bitter drugs needed for its treatment.

Those who have written Indian history have also split the periods of history in a very strange way. The first one ancient period, the second one Shaka-Hunanese invasion period, the third one Muslim period and the fourth one was British period. The basic details & information which is used for writing history, is essentially the descriptions narrated by foreign writers based on their migration, travelogues, case studies and research work. This theory, on the basis of uncharted and fabricated basis, had also been established by these historians that Indian content available for writing history was not reliable. Based on this, whatever books in history were written, were supposed to have more importance and prominence to those foreigners.

The depiction of our nationalist heroes, and their efforts and achievements has not been or very rarely mentioned in our history books. In the opinion of historians and writers with colonial mentality, India has been only a geographical entity. In such a situation, it was natural that in the history books, all about the nationalists who considered India as the motherland, who sacrificed their life for India were to be ignored completely. That is why in most of the history text books, all the important national heroes, such as Maharana Pratap, Guru Gobind Singh and Chhatrapati Shivaji, and more so, rebelled against Akbar and Aurangzeb were described very less. Any kind of respect and appreciation towards national heroes for their philosopher, hard work and efforts they made are almost missing in history books.

Tribal revolutionaries made remarkable movements in different parts of the country against British rule, but historians have neglected & ignored all these national incidences due to their prejudices and written history books on the view of colonial impact. If this will continue and the history of the great saints of the nation to be ignored, then the complex problems that have arisen in different regions, into the past 1000 years due to foreign slavery, and without resolving them, it will become difficult & important to set up India as a capable and prosperous nation.

Indian national heroes have not got proper respect and suitable place in Indian history. Historians affected by colonial rule did not allow the nation's heroes to be established as role model before the country, who had sacrificed everything for the country. People who emulate the so-called liberal and colonial rule in place of such Nation Heroes have become unessential part of history illogically. Due to this type of history, Indian citizens have neither inspired nor can they be in the future.

It is not mentioned in any Indian history textbook that Sardar Vallabhbhai Patel had resigned from the Cabinet on December 23, 1947, opposing monopoly and short-sighted attitude of Jawaharlal Nehru's Kashmir policy, but due to Mahatma Gandhi's hegemony Sardar Patel was constrained. While Patel was severely restless and anxious to strengthen the unity and integrity of newly freed country, at the same time, Nehru was just engaged, by fair or foul means, in polishing his image.

Every person should understand that lies, superstitions, and hypothetical things in the pages of history cannot avail permanent values for a long time. History, without any doubt, dig out the truth, mercilessly. In the meantime, many misleading things written in selfish manner are exposed by the inexorable hands of time. This is also very relevant in the context of the history of modern India.

The evaluation of the Indian freedom movement and its heroes has been particularly done by historians. Their faulty and biased evaluations has only made history of this important period of Indian freedom movement completely imbalanced and far away from the truth. Nehru was a committed freedom fighter and a strong Prime Minister of the country. Nehru remained the politically powerful Prime Minister of India for a long period of time. He had full influence and control over his party and he continued to work for one and a half decades on the highest policy decision-making of the nation without any challenge. During this period, many such works which were required for nation building could not be done, that was extremely important to do this in the initial years of independence. Nehru, who was under colonial hypnosis, always contempted the values inspired by nationalism and deliberately appointed followers of his ideology, in all the positions of national importance. With this, the entire academic and ideological system of India changed into Nehru's worship. In the important national posts and commissions related to history writing and academic research, Nehru's followers and the persons of colonial mindsets had always been appointed, and they all were remained involved in Nehru's false praise.

It is clear that the efforts that should have been made at the level of history and academic research in the first two decades of achieving independence in India were completely missed. As a result, the entire generation of the country became completely deprived of its own sense of duty in the process of national values, national ideas and nation building. Because of this, continuous process of nation building in India had stucked. Due to this the continuous process of nation building had broken. The biggest side effect of Indian education, which has been suffering from colonial hypnosis, has been that in today's scenario, any kind of thinking about the nation seems to be seen with great surprise and curiosity, whereas for any nation it should be very easy and normal

Creation of New India

behaviour. Surprisingly, in this country, people use to accept anti-national things comfortably, whereas show curiosity and eagerness for pro-nation things.

As a nation, nothing can be more than this deadly psychology, behaviour and thinking. Many facts and truths have been omitted in the history due to their biased attitude. Its effect is not only limited to the history books, but it has also deviated and confused the country's political, social and cultural life. Re-evaluation of history is always bitter. When fantasy, superstition and artificiality are displaced by reality and originality, then for some time it seems unbelievable, mentally violent, and merciless blow to the morality, but in the end the truth gets exposed in its actual and original form. Nehru's image has been narrated and mentioned in such a way, from curriculum to communication media, that even speaking about the truth and revealing facts seems as his criticism.

There are two important factors in the building of Nehru's personality. First– His education and initiation happened in the best institutes of Europe, therefore, the European philosophy, literature and view-point had a profound impact on his global philosophy. Second– The impact of Mahatma Gandhi. Although Nehru and Gandhi were having less similarity on ideological, behavioural and cultural level, but both of them were probably most closed to each other in their generations. Gandhi intervened many times to make Nehru's personality practical and to have good connection with Indian social life. Nehru also tried his level best to adopt Gandhi's suggestions and instructions as an obedient disciple.

In Nehru's personality, the mixed impact of colonialism and Gandhian is evident. An example of the 1920s can be taken here, when Pandit Nehru wrote a detailed letter to Mahatma Gandhi regarding national problems. Gandhiji was quite astonished and wrote him that this detailed letter did not mention about 'untouchability' which was much spread in Hindu society. Indeed, Nehru's politics and his thinking were merely an extension of his personality. His knowledge about the society was limited and despite his very strong and capable positions, no significant effort was made by him towards social improvement. Politically, he was a very ambitious, but his political roots and level of ideological thinking were weak. He was a good speaker and a charming personality and was always conscious of how to develop his personality more impressive. He was also widely popular due to the liberal image, but he did not have the same credibility and respect among freedom fighters, nationalists and revolutionaries who always put their life in danger, and suffered a lot of hardship and difficulties in the freedom movement of the country.

Extinction of mother tongue

In the Independent India, the Indian languages were also not given much importance and badly neglected, as that happened with the History. In these six decades of Independent India, there has been continuously a step-motherly behaviour towards Indian languages. Undoubtedly, language is the only medium of communication. The ease of language helps in its circulation and transmission. The work of creative exchanges from other languages has been done by almost all the languages of the world. Every year many new words are included in the English dictionary. Of course, that language flourishes internationally, which has the potential to absorb the success of other languages. Hindi language has also tried to get simplicity and integrity from all the other languages spoken in the subcontinent.

In India, there has been much contribution of Hindi cinema, television and other means of communication the promotion of Hindi language. Although private TV channels, in India, do not specifically offer any program on Hindi language and literature but Indian newspapers, media world and government broadcasting institutes have been working for the development of Hindi and including other Indian languages. Programs like Spell Bee and more are organized on American TV, which inspires children to develop

     Creation of New India

language accuracy. Such efforts are not being done in Indian media. Indian media and TV channels are more focused on their business and politics, and news and events related to sports and entertainment industries. For the development of Indian languages, such efforts are not being done diligently by them. No enough efforts are made for our children's language and cultural development. In Indian literature, especially Hindi literature, Indian TV channels and other communication channels must have at least one or two programs mandatory in a week. Bharatendu Harishchandra has rightly said, 'If progress is in our language, then we'll all set towards progress' (*Nijbhasha unnatiahe*, as unnato ko mool).

It is absolutely essential to pay attention to the development of our mother tongue and official language, because this is related to our self-respect and our basic identity. Hindi is the third most spoken language in the world, but it should be a matter of concern that there is no place for Hindi in the World wide trade. One of the main reasons for this is that Hindi today has neither become the language of science nor the language of modern career building topics and business. Hindi should get proper respect and prestige, and for this it is necessary that through this, large-scale employment should also be made available.

Hindi is a victim of many prejudices today. Most Hindi speakers in the country also suffer from prejudices and narrow perceptions of Hindi language. A software like Quillpad is the creative technological efforts, due to which the dominance of the Roman script on SMS and Whatsapp reduced. The facility of using various Indian languages on the Internet can also play an important role in reviving our languages in the coming days. Government of India should now take a resolution to develop and strengthen Hindi as a ritual. Indian citizens must also develop a sense of respect for our national language and other Indian languages.

Many developed and competent nations of the world have a clear national policy and pride for the national language. Many countries such as China, Japan, Korea, Spain, France, Germany have been able to make much progress only due to the strength of their languages. This is due to China's pride for its language that today the number of people learning Chinese language 'Mandarin' is increasing rapidly in the US. It is clear that in terms of language, China have not knelt before the English-controlled world community, whereas made itself so competent and able that today the western countries are also becoming tempted to learn Chinese language. China has its own search engine, which works only in Chinese language. China has not allowed social media working in English language, like Facebook, to enter their country. India can take inspiration from such an example. Indians must show such a strong will to develop their language. If others are not interested in learning our language, then why are we mentally suffering from slavery?

In the society, the impact of information, processing and technology is visible everywhere. With the effect of the Communication and Information Revolution, today the entire country is amazed. Everyone is keen to be versed with the medium of communication and technology. The time which the student after their study hours and the working people after their office hours used to develop their creativity in that remaining time, has now been completely shifted to information, techniques and modern communication medium. Often, it seems as if the information and technology are not for us, rather we have created ourselves for information technology, and have become slaves of it. Information technology itself is a device by itself, not practicable. On the contrary, today we have assumed it as vice-versa.

Today innovation, creativity and sensitivity are increasingly diminishing from our life due to the immaturity and inelegance of considering the instrument as practicable. In the era of 'email' and 'chatting', the art of letter writing is almost disappeared. By letter writing innovation and creativity of a person develops.

          Creation of New India

Proper communication of the feelings and values is possible only through a letter, not by the message. The revolution in information technology is not only spoiling the art of writing, but lot many other arts are also losing their existence due to its influence, which has resulted in great loss to the art of creativity.

Hindi is actually a sophisticated form of Vedic language. The journey of Sanskrit from Pali, Prakrit to Devanagari script is centuries old.

Hindi today has become the identity of Indian culture. Compared with any other country, India is having many complications in terms of mother tongue and local languages. In a country where example for changing of the language, after every 'four miles', is given, such complexities are inherently natural. At present, there are about two dozen official languages in the country and many are in a race of getting this status. It is clear that till now the Indians have not been able to unite under the frame of a recognized national language, and this has been the biggest reason for the decline of national language and other Indian languages. That is why Indian languages are disappearing in education and jobs.

In India, Sanskrit is not a colloquial language today, and there must be very few people who will be able to earn their livelihood through this language. Despite its affluence, Sanskrit has not been able to save its relevance. Sanskrit did not just disappear from the society, but it has been also replaced by foreign languages such as German, French, Korean, etc in school education. The Indian government will have to take concrete steps immediately to change this mismanagement. One of the major weaknesses of the CBSE board is that it has included Hindi and other Indian languages as a subject, but they have not yet been made the medium of study. The strange situation exists when Hindi and other Indian languages are more prone to colloquialism than English and can be more helpful for students to understand the subject matter. By studying Sanskrit just for two-three years hardly they could acquire any concrete knowledge about their culture. In order to gain the knowledge of the Vedas-Upanishads, students have to study Sanskrit in depth and in today's era, it is not possible that students are going to study Sanskrit deeply for reading Vedas and Upanishads and other ancient texts. For this, they have to be encouraged to study Sanskrit in schools and colleges, and even in universities also.

Our policy-makers should pay attention to this– why there is a shortage of those people who can study and contribute a lot to spread their culture in the country? It is the responsibility of the Government of India and the States to motivate and encourage people to study and research the cultural subjects in colleges or universities to save the country's cultural heritage. National language and Sanskrit should be an important aspect of this study.

Hindi: Carriers of Indianness

In fact, no nation can achieve a respectable and stable position in the world without its basic language. India's identity today is from Hindi in the whole world, and by making it powerful and popular, India is going to have its acceptance as a competent country on the international platform. It is a matter of misfortune that even after independence, enough efforts has not been put to develop Hindi in the country. Today Hindi and its related literature are facing many sort of changes. Current Hindi literature is also getting familiar with modernity and subsequent discussions.

Due to the excessive use of information technology and communication media Hinglish is growing up today with the efforts of the new generation of young people, and in the name of simplifying it, efforts are being made to develop Hindi similar to English. Sanskrit based Hindi is almost unintelligible so it is also out of use. Hindi is definitely the carrier of India's cultural heritage and treasure of social remembrance. It is an important 'window' for Indian knowledge enhancement, which is necessary to keep open. The nation believes that more serious approach will be adopted

 Creation of New India

towards the language in the future, and every effort will be made to set Hindi as a competent language very fast.

Being originated and raised in India, Hindi is definitely a part of the country's culture and it has been a major role in the formation of competent India. There are many composers such as Amir Khusro, Kabir, Soor, Tulsi, Jaaysi, Meera, Raidas, Ras Khan, Bharatendu, Premchandra, Prasad, Nirala, exist in Hindi language, despite obstacles of religion, caste and region, etc. Vallabhacharya, Ramanuj, Biththaldas, Ramanand, Swati Tirunal of Kerala, Saint Devraj of Maharashtra, Sahuji of Tanjore, Andal Purushottam of Machilipatnam composed verse in Hindi. Narsi Mehta of Gujarat, Namdev and Gyaneshwar of Maharashtra, Guru Nanak Dev of Punjab, Shankardev of Assam, Chaitanya Mahaprabhu of Bengal, Maharshi Dayanand of Gujarat and many Sufi saints also expressed their views using Hindi language to the people of the country.

Gandhi ji used Hindi as a common language for the part of the freedom movement. He himself wanted that the Hindi language should be simple, acceptable and technically effortless. In his words, Hindi is the name of that language, which Hindus and Muslims in India speak naturally effortless. There is no difference between Hindi and Urdu. When written in Devanagari, it is Hindi and when it is written in Persian script, it becomes Urdu.

On 14th September 1949, Indian Parliament had accepted Hindi as an 'official language'. Due to the colonial mindset and self-interest, Hindi has not been publicized and propagated to the desired level till date. In the context of language, the necessary guidelines are contained in article 343 of the Constitution as Official Language and are included in the 8th Schedule of the Constitution described in Article 351. Hindi is the mother tongue, literary language and ethnic language of almost 50 crore people. Many other languages written in Devanagari script are also closely related to Hindi. It is clear that Hindi has the power to add entire India in one source. There is a need to make extensive efforts in a planned manner to increase the reputation of Hindi at the international level. Many good efforts have also been made to develop and establish Hindi at the international level. Many organizations, litterateur and language lover have been offering their entire life for the development and enhancement of Hindi. Today, efforts are also being made to make Hindi adaptable in the new age of information and technology. Overseas Indians have a special role in the development of Hindi at the international level. They have made India's language culture vibrant and well-being outside India.

Many Hindi-language magazines and newspapers are also being published abroad. The 'Basant' of Mauritius, 'Purvaai' of England, 'Saurav' and 'Vishva Vivek' of America and 'Shantidoot' of Norway are particularly notable. Bilingual dictionaries of many languages have also been prepared. Many NRI writers are writing very important matter continuously. The exemplary thing is that most NRIs consider Hindi as a symbol of Indian identity. Many compositions have been translated into foreign languages. With the help of computers and the Internet, presence of Hindi on the global surface is steadily increasing, as it is evident from the initiative of Google as well. The e-versions of the newspapers are also releasing out. Today, Hindi is also being used in many countries like Thailand, United States and England, etc. In terms of numbers and acceptance, Hindi is the most spoken and used language in the world today after the Chinese and English languages. In the past few years, from the point of view of literature, Hindi language has become creative, flexible and communicative. Hindi is becoming effective in the medium of communication. The areas of its use have increased and the expression power has expanded.

○

 Creation of New India

3

Inferiority in Reference to Language

Hindi was established by the Indian Constitution as the official language of the Union. Before the constitution was passed in English, the consent was agreed upon for the first 15 years as the language of the state after the constitution was enacted in independent India. It was also made that if necessary, the Indian Parliament could extend the use of English in the form of the language of the government by making a law for a period of 15 years. This provision shows that the Indian Constitution makers and policy makers wanted that the use of English as the language of the successive years and the reliance on it gradually decreases year after year and in this period Hindi should be adequately enabled and developed in the form of national language, so that all the policy, administrative and legal work can be easily done in Hindi.

To do this, the policy instructions were also made clear under Article 351 of the Indian Constitution, according to which it will be the duty of the Union, to publicized Hindi and to make its overall development, so that it could become the proper medium of expression of all the elements of India's social culture. It was also instructed that without the linguistic interference in it, it is mainly used for assimilation of the forms, styles and positions of other languages of India specified in 'Hindustani' and the eighth list. If it is necessary or desirable, for storing its words, then get the words from Sanskrit and other languages, ensure its prosperity.

Of course, the principle of constitution makers cannot be doubted to establish Hindi language as a national language and to enhance its overall form. In fact, in the first decade of independent India, English speakers were sitting on high positions in the Union's governance and administration system. In the Indian armed forces, law and business sectors, there was dominance of English linguistic people with colonial hypnosis. The hidden agenda of this class was something else. These people were not serious about implementing the provisions of the Indian Constitution. They were hypnotized by English language and were used to of this language.

It is absolutely essential to pay attention to the development of our mother tongue and official language, because this topic is related to our self-respect and our basic identity. Hindi is the third most spoken language in the world, but it should be a matter of concern that there is no place for Hindi in the world trade. One of the main reasons for this is that Hindi today has neither become the language of science nor has it become the language of modern career building topics and business. Hindi should get proper respect and prestige, for this it is necessary that through this, large-scale employment should also be made available.

The mental slaves of colonial civilization, in the entanglement of foreign language, had forgotten their mother language, culture and identity long ago. This class received complete protection from the powerful independent India and Prime Minister Jawaharlal Nehru. It is clear that after attaining independence, whatever efforts should have been made to communicate nationalist values in India and whatever effective steps should be taken in this direction, nothing has been done. Certainly India missed this very rare and precious opportunity due to short-sightedness. This type of national treason cannot be forgiven.

In order to keep their hold on important positions of government machinery and profit due to their colonial mental slavery and selflessness, the fierce anti-national people put the fate of millions of

Indians and the respect of the nation on risk forever. In independent India, Nehru's followers continued with the stealthy movements about the language. The interest of English continues to be consistent even on the basis of nationwide conflicts on the reorganization of states on linguistic basis. In independent India so far, the English linguists remained the dominant influence and they considered themselves to be the 'destiny of the nation' and 'policy dictators' of the nation. This class deliberately created many countries, sections and sects within one India for its own benefit.

Market of Languages

The language field has become a huge business at present. Seeing the great business success of English as a result of the English-language policy, French, German and Spanish languages are continuously engaged in making efforts to increase their share in India. Foreign governments are preparing a prospective learner for their universities by making a place for their language in our schools. These learners by spending huge foreign currency travel abroad for studying. Many advertisements from foreign educational institutions coming out daily in Indian media and newspapers attract Indian students. Many advertisements from foreign educational institutions that appear daily in Indian media and newspapers attract Indian students. Since many universities of England and America have attracted millions of Indian students, they have started earning billions of dollars, since then other European countries are also making continuous efforts to attract many Indian students. If Indian students will study German, then they will go to Germany for higher education. This policy of developed nations is causing serious damage to Indian education and knowledge. India should no longer ignore national interest in the field of education.

Due to ideological hypocrisy in India, there has been a lot of misery in Indian education and Indian languages. This misery is still going on. It is the misfortune of our languages that speaking in its favor is called 'backwardness', whereas foreign languages are given the status of being 'modern' in the society. Continuous misleading propaganda has been carried out in the context of Indian languages, in a thought-provoking strategy. Often Sanskrit is linked to Hinduism and it is presented as a communal language. Today, the whole world needs to be told that Sanskrit was a great language of knowledge and till date. It can be easily experienced by reading Sanskrit texts and Sanskrit literature. There is so much attraction of the Sanskrit language that even the staunch anti-secular always prefer to keep Sanskrit-inspired names of their children. For Sanskrit language, there has always been a attraction and respect in the mind of country's thinkers. It cannot be denied that Sanskrit language itself is a vision and carrier of ancient Indian civilization, culture, philosophy, art and literature.

During the freedom movement, the top national leaders and mentors of the country like Tilak, Rabindranath Thakur, Mahatma Gandhi, Sri Arvind and others urged that Sanskrit is the mother of all the regional languages developed in India from time to time. The gateway to ancient language which awakens Indian self-realization can be only Sanskrit language. Gandhi ji used to say that every Indian should learn Sanskrit language. He used to say that it is necessary for Muslims and Christian children also to get Sanskrit education. In 1930, Gandhi ji encouraged Sardar Patel and all other colleagues in jail for reading Sanskrit. This illustration is safe in the correspondence of Gandhi ji and Mahadev Bhai's diary. The so-called elites who gave importance to the German language instead of Sanskrit, are not aware of the history of India, nor do they have any concern and worry about national unity and national pride.

In the form of oriental science, research and study are going on by various universities on different aspects of Sanskrit, but neglecting it in India is a matter of concern. In India, the main cause of the misery of Sanskrit language is the illusion, rumor and inferiority of Sanskrit, and it is considered as very age old. It is being considered as a matter of museum and an object of historical significance. Considering Sanskrit as a threat to pseudo-secularism, actually not based on facts, is a very conservative conception. In India, this malady towards Sanskrit is also preoccupied with bias and political reasons. Losing Sanskrit will mean that the country is deprived of the ancient Indian vast knowledge assets.

Language is not merely a mechanism of mere letter or word store. It brings with it many thoughts and philosophy. An approach of seeing the world and society is also provided by the language. Surely the language has been the 'invention' of man's best and highest importance so far on this earth. Only by maintaining the heritage of Sanskrit, India can save its originality. Through Indian languages, India will be able to make a meaningful presence in contemporary discussions on the global stage. It cannot be disagreed that the basis of Indian culture and civilization is Sanskrit language itself. The texts like Vedas, Upanishads, which are considered to be the identity of India, have been written in Sanskrit language and no one can understand the wisdom of these texts without knowing the Sanskrit language. As the expansion of Sanskrit diminished over the time, so as Vedas-Upanishad texts also disappeared from the memory of people. As a result, our society is deprived of getting full benefit of these texts which are full of information, knowledge about ancient Indian culture.

It is true that there may be some complexities of Sanskrit language, but, is there any language in the world, in which there are no complications? In India, Sanskrit has always been seen by adding to the rampant discrimination and hypocrisy in the society. Due to these assumptions, the desired benefit of knowledge available in Sanskrit has not yet been get to the Indian society and the nation. Sanskrit has gradually lost its identity. Prior to the Mughal rule, Sanskrit was a widely popular in reading and writing, and in Indian society as well. With the passage of time, the growing influence of Arabic-Persian affected Sanskrit and it slowly moved out. In the Mughal rule, the official language was Arabic-Persian, so it is natural that the language which gets government support and protection, flourishes faster than other languages.

Last year, in November 2014, the government had issued mandatory instruction   to teach Sanskrit instead of German as a third language from class 6th to 8th. Some parents challenged this order in the Supreme Court, in turn the Supreme Court had asked for a reply from the government. The government clearly said that after considering all aspects, it has been decided to teach Sanskrit instead of German. While doing so, it has been kept in mind that neither the children have any additional burden nor their interests get affected. Therefore, this year only the basics of Sanskrit will be taught. The children who are in class 8th, they will also be taught only the basic Sanskrit of 6th standard, so that they will not be burdened.

The assessment of children from class 6 to 8 is done only by same school teachers. Outside teachers do not assess them. In such a situation, they do not have to worry. Children who want to pursue a career on German language, their interests will not be affected, as German can be read as an additional subject. Thus, the interest of 74 thousand children studying German in 504 central schools will not be affected. Out of these, 24 thousand children are studying German as an additional subject only. The government has said that so far, German languages was being taught, Central School Organization and the Maxmular Building. This Agreement expired on September 2014 and the Government has not renewed it in national interest. It is clear that if India has to be strong and powerful, then it is must to make Indian languages and education self-sufficient and self-respecting.

Technology affects languages

New information technology and Internet are today the major source of global knowledge. No language can be empowered in the present era, unless its extensive use is on Internet. Figures show that currently 55.8% of the content available on the internet is in the English language, whereas only 5% of the world's population uses English as their first language. Only 21% of the people in the world understand English. Compare to this, the languages like Arabic or Hindi, which are widely spoken in the world, their Internet content is available only 0.8 and 0.1 % respectively. In the past few years, the Internet and various social networking sites have emerged as the medium of expression, hopes and expectations which is remarkable. Indeed, in India, Internet can be provided with speed and popularity only when its majority of content be in Hindi and other regional languages. Hindi and other Indian languages will have to be promoted on Internet, then only non-English speaking will join Internet more. Although, the scope of the expansion of Hindi and other regional languages is still limited to Internet search and voice search, hopefully the effect of this experiment will be in every area of life. The biggest benefit of this will be to the farmers living in rural areas, because on the Internet, the material is not available in Hindi or other regional languages and their English knowledge is almost negligible.

In the global market today English is dominated as a contact language, but most of the countries in the world are not only working in their own language but also feel pride for that. Today, in the world, most of the people use Mandarin language. They mainly live in China, Taiwan, Singapore, Malaysia etc. After this, the most spoken language in the world is Hindi, the people of India, Nepal, Fiji, Mauritius speak Hindi, but, in our country, there is one, so called, aristocratic class which keeps inferior feelings towards Hindi.

It is astonishing that the number of English speaking people is only 5.43% in the world, but the dominion of this language has been proved on the entire global system. Of course, this achievement is the result of their hard work and continuous innovative research in the field of technology. Why not consider this achievement in India as an inspiration; and we can make our mother tongue capable, popular and empowering. Ironically, India's affluent, competent, and so called elite class is against our own Indian languages. Due to this, Indian languages are not able to develop and also not getting that acceptance, popularity and respect. This conspiracy against Indian languages should be considered as an anti-national activity.

German is ranked 11th in the most spoken languages in the world, but the elite Indian and our policy makers, are giving priority to the German language over Sanskrit, which carries our ancient traditions. In fact, such people are Manasaputra of Macaulay-Marx. The education system of this country is being pursued by Macaulay's policy, which had implemented the English medium in the country's education and governance system for the purpose of administering British colonial interests. His plan was to create such a pseudo-and-rooted Indian class with English language and western living, which not only favors the British at the local level, but also retains the colonial system in India for an indefinite period.

After independence, the education and governance system prevailing in the English colonial era should have been changed immediately, but it was not done that way. Macaulay's Manasaputras proved their devotion to the colonial system in place of this nation. Nehru, who considered himself to be an Englishman at the mental and ideological level, did not consider the importance of Bhartiya in Indian education and governance system. He entrusted the country's top educational regulatory institutions and the administrative system of the country in such hands, which were almost unaware of the culture and patriotism, and remained confined to mere anglo-ideology. Due to the contaminated conduct of these Manasaputras of Macaulay, India could never been established on the global stage as a dignified nation. Whatever improvement has been in academic field in India, after Independence, is mostly due to the contribution of our nationalist thinkers.

Should we ignore the people who are living in millions of villages of Indian states like Bihar, Uttar Pradesh, Jharkhand, Rajasthan, Haryana and and billions of people who read in their own language, on the grounds that they don't know English? Is it not the action taken against the basic rights of the citizens? Is it the English language only privilege on knowledge, skill or intelligence? The logic of English speakers is also baseless that the language of law and technology, in the world, is only English. Are the countries like Germany, Japan, China, Korea and France not doing all the tasks related to law, administration, technology and research in their national languages successfully? Indeed, the basic reason of the progress of these countries has been that they have done all the above mentioned work in their own national language. That is why every citizen of these countries feels their connectivity and sense of responsibility pertaining to national policies and duties. Unfortunately, if this has not been done in India, then the main historical reason behind this is the continuous ignorance and insult of Indian languages.

The number of English speaking people in the country is only 2 crores, and with this India cannot become a global superpower. It is clear that India's growth is inherent and secure only in the development of Indian languages. Now the time has come for Indian citizens to think about this situation, who always talk about nationalism. If the present curriculum prevailed in Indian education and the current textbooks of children and other study materials should be visualized, it automatically becomes clear how is English going to swallow all Indian languages in the name of modern education? Is this the identity of a self-respecting and independent nation? Did millions of revolutionaries and patriots sacrifice their lives for achieving the goal of independent India only to maintain this kind of 'ideological slavery' and frustrated mentality? Does a vast independent nation like India today have not been able to honor its mother tongue? Is India so poorly rooted that cannot develop its own languages and cannot make them worth to study and conduct research, development, science, technology, administration and law in their own language.

It is ridiculous that after doing most or complete studies in their own Indian languages, many people start trying to speak in English, after sitting in important positions. Indian administration, Indian judicial system and Indian policy planning are till now all linguistically under slavery. This kind of mental slavery has put India such a big nation down too much. The sooner the situation changes, the better it will be for the country.

Indian languages: Neither in education, nor in jobs

The birth of Hindi movement, in India, was not in Hindi-speaking areas, but in non-Hindi speaking provinces like Bengal, Maharashtra and Gujarat. The great thinkers of Bengal like Rajendra Lal Mitra, Keshavchandra Sen, Bhudev Mukhopadhyay and Naveen Chandra Das rewarded and recommended Hindi as a communication language. Swami Dayanand implemented the Devanagari script for Marathi language, but after getting independence, the question of language has become a subject of more employment and livelihood than nationalism.

The non-Hindi speakers having their regional languages were of the opinion that if English was replaced by Hindi as an official language in work, then their language would be lagged behind in competing education and employment. In order to honour this feeling, Trilingual Formula was created in the country, in which up to the 8th standard, Hindi and English were urged to learn compulsory languages along with learning any of the regional languages, especially a South Indian language. This formula was approved in the National education schemes implemented in the years 1968, 1986, 1992 etc.

If India has to be established as a global superpower, then it must make its own language fully competent and prosperous up to the level of international standards and innovative communication technique technology essentially. Just as developed and capable countries like France, Germany, Japan, China, Korea, Holland, Spain, and Russia are carrying out their work of scientific research and technical competence in their national language. In these countries, the national language is being used in the administrative and judicial system. It is a matter of surprise that India still has not understood the meaning and importance of the pride of its languages. There is as such no environment in the country in the direction of self-reliance on language. It seems that due to the slavery and colonial rule of thousands of years, we have not yet recovered from the hypnosis of foreign languages. In India, even today, Indian languages are being considered not only as of second standard, and are also being proven the same at every stage of policy formation, as well.

O

4

Competent Language, Competent Nation

In India, students are being attracted towards learning foreign languages to make their careers. There is no harm in this, but it should not be done at the cost of our own languages. The department of foreign languages such as German, Japanese, and Chinese etc. can be created easily at the university level, but teaching these languages at the school level will be illogical. In independent India, rather we should have tried to make free our Indian society, administration, judicial system, education, research and technology, and media sector, from the cluster of English language.

At the level of the language, if India continues to behave in a disgraceful state of inferiority complex, then in future, it may face more critical situation. In future if Japan, China or France also insist on teaching their languages in Indian schools and we continue to fulfill their insistence, will it not be an injustice to our educational system and children? The need to learn an important lesson in the Indian context is that for the continued expansion of its language and culture, Germany has inflicted its full strength in dialogue, discussions and decision making in India, due to its language love. India has certainly never made efforts at this level for its fundamental Indian languages. Indeed, in India, it has been behaving exactly the opposite.

Creation of New India

While many developed countries of the world struggle to live and die for their languages, but this glorious feeling has not yet been created in India in their language. It is a unfortunate fact that today Indian languages are neither left in education, nor they have any future in jobs. As a nation we have been constantly ignoring the topics which should really be a matter of pride for us. As a nation, we have actually done nothing to empower our language and culture. India is the only such unfortunate nation in the world, which is not worried about its 'national identity'. In the case of language for hundreds of years India has actually been performing psychological slavery and inferiority complex. It is beyond the understanding that why can't we give our mother tongue the essential glory and cannot develop it overall?

Young India

According to United Nations Population Fund, the total population of youth in the age group of 10 to 24 years has reached 1.8 billion in the world. Today, the world's most populous country of youth has become India. In India, if immediate strong steps are not taken in the right direction to fulfill the basic needs, employment opportunities and aspirations of this vast young population, then unemployment and other serious problems associated with it will get formidable in the country. The power of youth should be involved in nation-building, not in the anti-national and anti-social work, for this, the young population will have to provide better opportunities to move forward and live happily in life.

This is certainly the first opportunity in the history of human civilization, when such a vast young population is available to India. In India, the total population of people aged below 25 years has crossed 60.5 million. This population is more than the entire population of Europe. Obviously, to take advantage of this huge youth population, we have to deal with the challenges like education, health, skill development and employment generation.

In view of the present Indian resource capacity, there is a need to work on a comprehensive and concerted strategy immediately to deal with this challenge. Indian experience reveals that every year a situation of fierce conflicts arises in the students for admission in the best schools. Even meritorious students with 90 percent marks cannot get admission in the desired colleges due to huge competition. It cannot be said that the students who did not get admission in the good schools lacked any kind of talent.

The truth is that there is still enough number of good and world-class schools in India that cannot be built. Because of this, crores of young people have to suppress their desires to get better education every year. It is not only their own personal harm, but the society and the nation which is deprived of their talent is also greatly harmed. Why can't it be that in the proportion of the number of students, in each district, town and city of the country by planning a minimum of 1 or 2 world class schools specializing in arts, commerce, science, technology, management and technology? This will enable a better environment of education together in the entire country and in the absence of resources and opportunities; there could be no injustice done with the country's talent. Given the world-class school at the local level, the talent of remote areas of India facing the problem of resources will also be benefitted greatly by this process.

The way in which education has become highly commercialized in the present time, it is becoming very difficult to achieve higher and professional education for the poor and unemployed youth. In education, if a class is going to be established on the basis of money, then nothing more will be worse than this for the society and the nation. International Labor Organization (ILO) estimates that by 2020, 11.6 million people in the age group of 20 to 24 will become part of the working population.

Every year more than 10 million new people stand in line of employment in India, whereas in the last 10 years, only 15 million

Creation of New India

new jobs have been created. Due to the increasing competition for opportunities, among the Indian youth, psychological struggles on the basis of gender and class inequality are increasing. Many times it has come to notice that among the young people, many types of political, social classes have got ready and they are struggling with mutual interests.

These kinds of conflicts are arising due to the lack of resources and opportunities. Misuse of this kind of youth power is very harmful for the nation. Due to the increasing unemployment and lack of opportunities and incentives, millions of Indian youth are compelled to waste their time in vain.

From villages to towns and cities, billions of Indian youths are wasting their precious time in the useless work and merely gossips. The crowd of these youths is visible everywhere, on public rallies, political rallies, unproductive demonstrations, alleged spiritual and religious events, generally held in every nook and corner of the country, at all times. Crores of Indian youth, who are struggling with opportunities and lack of motivation, get involved in these futuristic events and organizations to find a proxy and transient psychological relief of 'finding a meaningful purpose' for their own life. In order to deal with these many challenges, it is essential that the strategists, without any further delay, prepare a solid strategy to make the youth efficient, educated, and innovative.

Undoubtedly, the present era is the age of 'knowledge' and 'innovation'. The vast youth population is like an opportunity for India. If India could make its youth technically and educationally sound and skillful, surely it could be established in the form of a technically efficient global superpower within a decade. If 60 crore youths of the country are joined together for nation's building in a constructive manner, in the right direction, enthusiastically then soon the country can be rejuvenated.

All the Indian Prime Ministers so far have been talking of representing a vast young country at international forums, but no clear 'youth policy' that encourages education, employment and entrepreneurship has been created in the country till date. In the year 2012, The Government of India had the point of making a Youth Development Index in the draft Youth Policy, but there was no planned schematic explicit strategy in this direction that could be kept before the country. In spite of numerous efforts, there is truth and fact that around 1.13 crore Indian youth join the growing row of unemployed people looking for job every year and kept increasing year by year. Most of them have no opportunity for proper development and creative use of their talents and abilities.

It is also an irony that Indian education is still being running on an age-old tradition. After 20 years of continuous study, when Indian youth put step in the field of employment and other enterprises, they realize that whatever they have been studying till now, have no practical use anywhere. Indian education has been completely restricted in scoring marks somehow by just memorizing the books. It does not have the capability of basic knowledge and practical use.

Indian education is not able to encourage hard work, experimentalism, creativity and originality. This is the reason that most Indian youth cannot take courageous decisions related to creativity and entrepreneurship in their lives and somehow they are forced to live their life by doing just job. Indian education is not able to make our youth psychologically capable of making self-reliant and courageous decisions.

Statistics show that less than three percent of the students in India are those who have got any vocational education at high school level. The opportunity to continue higher education is only one out of every five students passing the primary class. In India, there are even fewer young people with capital, skills and other necessary resources to start any business or venture in India. Crores of Indian youth are becoming victims of hopelessness and depression, due to not getting any work of their choice with two to three years after the completion of education or discontinued. Although there are so many reasons to be unemployed, but the major cause is their 'inefficiency or unskilledness'. Crores of Indian youth want to see themselves, their society and country, to be better and stronger. The country should also equip its younger generation with education, health, skill, employment, entrepreneurship, social values and resources.

5

Indian Media

As a nation we often show our inferiority complex. Due to this kind of conduct, we are being pulled on the global stage. Over the last several decades, Indian politicians have been visiting different conferences and events abroad on most occasions, but they are not given any special place or importance often by the global media. Even from different programs to the media reports, even their names are not correctly spoken, but nothing is taken seriously in those countries and our system, as well.

On the contrary, when foreign leaders visit our country, we get highly excited and put our best in welcoming them. Despite, most of them do not have even any kind of loyalty towards India. Recently when China's President Shi Jinping came to India, an Indian television anchor lost his job, only because that he could not correctly pronounce the name of the Chinese President. The behaviour with this kind of inferiority complex cannot be appreciated.

It is also a matter of great concern that the Indian media has been entangled in the instant, illogical and short-sighted news content that caters only its own business interests and spreads its excitement. Due to Fierce Competition of the media groups, the attention of Indian media has the intellectual issues of national importance. In most of the media organizations the journalists who are working, are not formally or informally trained. India still lacks world-class research institutes in the field of journalism. For business reasons, the Indian media is still entangled in the TRP network. Twenty-four-hour news channels are running from morning till late at night, but they do not have any high level content and matured news to show. Indian media is still giving more importance to 'shortcut' ways to attract public attention. Because of this, the Indian public don't get matured and creative news and information.

Indian media mostly focus more on the news, which happens around the metros of Delhi and Mumbai. Since the offices of most of the media institutions are established in these cities, it is more comfortable, economical and accessible to cover these news. The incidents related to crime, always given priority and importance and suddenly created as a national incident by the news channels. Often, incidents related to crimes are broadcasted in such a sensational manner that the incident and its related 'follow up' can be presented in new colorful manner for successive days to come. Many times, Media Trial of this type kills the fundamental rights of many citizens and also affects the judicial procedure widely. Many times, this type of Media Trial is also creative; many times this unnecessary Media Trial is no longer harmless. Due to this, quality investigation in many cases hampered.

Hunting a dead person

Many times it has also been seen that after media dignified the so-called influential people and the activities related to them, later, if there is any exposure of their involvement in certain matters, the media immediately takes a U-turn towards those persons and activities related to them. It should be asked that when the media had been aware of such influential persons and activities related to them, so why did not they expose such malicious activities at that time? Why the media suddenly start attacking only when investigating agencies begin to take action? This awkward behavior of the media is like 'Hunting a dead person'. Indian media cannot gain respect with this kind of behaviour. Media should also become the medium of expression of the suffering of millions of deprived masses living in remote areas of entire India. If the media hangs around only some capable and influential people of the country, how will they be able to fulfill their fundamental obligations?

Such interest to cover criminal incidents occurring in remote rural areas of India often is not shown by news channels. Many editions are published from different states in the print media. Due to regional issues being published, newspapers often give special importance to local news related to public interest in local edition. In contrast, most of the news channels do a single broadcast at the national level. Due to this, Indian news channels could not make proper balance between the news of national importance and regional news related to local problems. In such a case, news channels also try to see how news should be expanded in an interesting and sensational way that for many days they can become the basis of curiosity for the whole country as well.

Making mountain out of a mole-hill

It can also be seen in India that dozens of news channels are continuously engaged in this effort every day to make some topic, statements or any incidence for discussion by involving some personality of this nature. This type of controversial statement provides news channels to engage the country in 'prime time' for many days.

Many times, due to the ego of their personal interests and 'power performance' by the media in unnecessary and irresponsible manner, the 'talking/discussion of the matter' remains. Even at the time of Nirbhaya Incident, this trend of Indian news channels and their tendency to confuse national public opinion was clearly revealed. The news channels kept sniffing throughout the country for a number of days even after the big scandal, who were those important persons celebrating the New Year's party or those who had been seen, laughing

　　　　　　　　　　　　　　　　Creation of New India

and enjoying in a normal way? These news channels should be asked that if they are really so distraught and vulnerable to the Nirbhaya incident and the same many criminal acts that happen every day in India, so why did not they stop their advertising and financial contracts for a few minutes in mourning?

Resources and power are actually the objects of utilization. The tendency to make pressure by misusing resources and power cannot be said to be fair. The media's attitude is that 'we have the stage, we will show whatever we want and will present, whatever we want to' is totally unfavorable in the spirit of our jurisdiction and civil liability. Media and press are actually the mirror of the society and they should work in this form only. The media wants to adopt the role of the 'designer' or 'self-made judge' of society, forcefully, which is not fair. This suggestion from Markandey Katju is appropriate that even professional and specialist education must be made mandatory for journalists.

The real issues are different

In Indian democracy, the media has been approved as an important pillar. Indian diplomats and the President, the Prime Minister, the Vice President and the Union Ministers etc. have to take the media along with them during foreign visits. It is essential that Indian journalists must have adequate knowledge of Indian constitution, parliamentary system, democratic system, rule and law, science and technology, and society and administration. Without this knowledge, Indian media will generally remain a victim of 'low profile'. At this moment, the Indian news channel is a victim of 'cheap' and 'shallow'. It appears that, somehow they have to pass the time only.

In the morning, religious discourses, followed by fitness programs, programs related to cooking, recording of various soap operas on television (The illogical serials that continues till eternity), Bollywood news, comedy show etc. are the ways for passing time. In the evening, a few leaders gather and discuss mostly on controversial topics on prime time. These debates do not provide any benefit at the national level. Often nothing is achieved by the people of the country watching these futile TV debates. It seems that most of the Indian news channels change in the evening; they become confined in the form of arguments and resolving disputes. At 11 pm, news channels are handed over to some baba, tantric, astrologers and tele-shopping agencies, who are engaged in efforts to make millions of people 'fool' till morning.

Every day, these News channels are remained restless for 'breaking news' for every hours. Many times, even in claiming this, the news channels work day and night so that they should get such stories, breaking news and use to claim to be the first. Most news channels start behaving as 'self-made higher court and judge'. Anchors often talk less, and fight more with the visitors and the guests. Their restlessness prevails over why the invited guest is not saying that, which they wants.

Clearly, the Indian media has not yet matured completely and it's ideological and knowledge level is still not enough. It certainly is very important in building the nation. The Indian media should discharge its responsibility more seriously and whatever allegations they are facing should be resolved.

Today, the English media is creating a feeling of 'cultural and psychological degradation' around the world. This has made 'consumerism' a sense of reputation for the whole world. In the less developed countries, its promotional mechanism, the strong marketing network and the English language have developed such an environment that is based on the sale and copying of the products of Western countries, it has come into self-employment to give civilization certificates to other countries and its citizens. With the help of efficient marketing, foreign media and multinational industrial houses are increasingly pushing their poor goods in the poor and underdeveloped countries with great earnings.

 Creation of New India

Even in India, junk food, unhealthy pizzas, burgers, hot dogs and confectionery products are being sold here, in a big way, whereas Indian snacks and Street food which are best suited to Indian conditions and very healthy, despite all the merits, don't exist in the absence of good marketing.

Mental slavery

Indian society still couldn't come out of the clutches of colonial mental slavery. Every area of Indian society is entangled in this mental slavery. Indian media has also not been able to be completely Bharatiya due to this colonial slavery. Especially the English media is a victim of being its follower.

Today, it is the fact that we may not have any news of our country, even if we are unaware of the important national issues and key persons of the country, but our English newspaper keeps on telling us about 70 pages every day that what are even the ordinary artists doing in Hollywood movies and their TV shows, what are they wearing, what are they eating, and who are they? It should really be a matter of shame for us as a citizen, how we are being psychologically dominated by the western countries. This is when, in India, the experimental efforts are being made in more cultural, creative and art fields than in these countries.

English language and English media have completely established control over our thinking. Especially the youth class of the country is unnecessarily engaged in getting directions from them. This has lost our originality and uniqueness and we have become slaves of consumerism. There can be no greater sin than this that you get separated from your original identity and your roots. Do not respect it and go on condemning and criticizing it. World over, in the developed countries, Media has played very important role for the unity in society and restoration of their country. Unfortunately, the Indian media has not been able to achieve this type of maturity right now.

India's English media is deeply mislead and a slave of western culture. In India, the English media has always been cherished and flourished by rich industrial houses and multinationals, therefore, it usually does not endanger the risk of any financial crisis. While working in India due to being financially prosperous and self-reliant, it does not have any concern with Indian values. It appears that it is only employed in India as an agent of Western countries. Not surprisingly, a part of the English media is supporting the Kiss of Love pridefully. It is promoting kissing in public places like birthright. This is the same media, which considers 'drinking alcohol' a national right.

The misfortune of this country is that the English media does not associate itself with the mentality and interest of this country, nor it has any such aim. The absurdity of Western artists, who are addicts with shamelessness, the English media, which is serving daily in front of the Indian public, separates itself from the subjects of national pride. The English media, which operates on Western money, presents a variety of Western artists in the form of a model and 'icon' in front of the country.

More recently, the two great personalities of the country, Madan Mohan Malviya and Atal Bihari Vajpayee, were embellished with the Bharat Ratna, the country's highest Civilian award, but the main English newspapers of India could not find any space in the entire newspaper to mention about them, because the entire space of these newspapers is consumed in the commercials of the horror and degraded artists of the West and the advertisements of consumer products. India's English media remains as conscious and vigilant about the freedom of expression, the freedom to live a clean life, the rights of homosexuals and the display of the fashion and body of the western artists, that's not actively showcase the basic problems of India.

Well, it would have been possible that some arrangements have been made to put an end to the anti-national media of this kind, which is acting in the name of 'freedom of expression' to seduce and mislead the people of the country.

Begging from beggars

Whenever there is talk of the quality of communication mediums in India, it often proves that Indian citizens are not hard working and serious in terms of 'creativity'. What is the reason that Indian citizens are being attracted to TV and TV programs that are mostly entertaining? Most of the Indian TV channels continue to show entertaining programs and endless serials all day long. Their increasing TRP indicates that Indian viewers prefer such an interesting entertaining and light program. What is the reason that Indian audiences have a huge lack of interest in international issues of importance and interest in research related to environment and science. In India, TV channels such as BBC, CNN, Discovery, History channels have not been developed yet.

The question arises: Are the Indian viewers only addicted to shallow entertainment and light information materials? Some time ago, China had excluded many foreign programs broadcast on television in their country from 'prime time' broadcast. The purpose behind this was to promote domestic entertainment and industry there. Though this dictum dictates China's dictatorship behind this decision, but its concern for the promotion of the culture and entertainment industry of its own country can not be underestimated. India should also take inspiration from them, but unfortunately in India it is happening exactly its opposite. In India, the supremacy of foreign media groups is already established. Most of the indigenous programs and perceived reality shows shown on TV have actually became fake and shallow imitation or indigenous versions of America and other foreign programs.

Almost all reality shows broadcast in India are merely copies of shows of some foreign channels. For example, 'Kaun Banega Crorepati' (Who Wants To Become Millionaire), 'Comedy Night

With Kapil' (The Kumars), 'Big Boss' (Big Brother), 'Indian Idol' (American's Idol), 'India's Got Talent' (America's Got Talent), 'Master Chef' (Master Chef Australia), 'Is jungle se mujhe bachaao' (I Am A Celebrity - Get Me Out of Here), Or 'Khatron ke Khiladi' (Fear Factor) etc. Most of these shows have been copyrighted, and while the original concept of some foreign shows have been stolen and produced.

This type of trend proves that the Indian entertainment industry is not quite creative and hard working. It is a matter of surprise that the nation, which has given a great talent in art, culture, literature and cinema, has become 'pauper' in ideological and creative form that it has to borrow creativity and innovation from them, who are not in a position to give themselves some good and creative. Indian media and entertainment industry is displaying behavior like 'begging from beggars'.

○

   Creation of New India

6
Value of Life

At present, the modern world is facing many problems like war, terrorism and violence etc. If we look into them carefully, these problems are actually been created by us. The universal truth is that our life progresses with the attachment, cooperation and mutual community relations to each other. Various international contracts, bilateral agreements and United Nations declarations proclaim this unity and sense of equality. India has made unique contribution in this matter. The wonderful initiatives of ideas, science and development that make man better here are continuing. All the ancient philosophies, religions, traditions and ideas here are basically putting emphasis on peace of mind and spiritual prosperity.

Thoughts of Sankhya and Yoga, Justice, Universal Meteorology, Vedanta and Charvak Traditions have been equally purposeful to make humans happy and upgraded. Traditions and philosophy of China and Egypt have also really worked in this direction. In spite of all this, there is no doubt that India's contribution at the level of world peace and tolerance has been of paramount importance in the world. Hindutva and Buddhism are the gifts of this world to India, who first presented unity, peace and equality in front of the world as an ideal way of conduct. Indeed, there is no conceptual difference in Buddhism and Hinduism. Both emphasize equanimity, peace and wisdom equally on the purity of morality, concentration and intelligence.

Panchamahants are synthesized in the womb of the human body created by the sky, air, fire, water, and earth elements. There is constant change in the human body created with these five elements. He gets younger from the child, young man, and then gets older. In the end, the same body gets merged into the Panchamahants. Similarly, the changes in the seasons also change over time. All types of mechanisms and their interconnected changes manifested by nature reveal the human dependence and interdependence. It is clear that unity and equality can only be a peaceful society and structure of a systematic world.

It is very necessary that human society is based on equality and justice. Equality of opportunity means, to remove all obstacles that obstruct individual self-development. This means that all the profession or business should be open to any talented person and should be based on progress, opportunities, qualifications. Social status, family relationships, social background and other such factors should not be interfered. Equality expects this that let any person start life in a level sports venue. The underlying assumption is that since the competition has been fair, the benefit itself has gone beyond criticism. There is no doubt that such a system will give birth to such people who will pay attention only to their talents and personal qualities.

Resistance and retribution of any kind of exploitation should be universal. Exploitation is intellectually, mentally, physically, economicaly, socially and culturally present in India from ancient times and despite six decades of constitutional social-political reform oriented efforts of independent India, India has not been fully absorbed in totality today.

Mental and intellectual exploitation produces a special kind of hypnosis, that the person does not even feel his pain and misery. Throughout exploitation and religious rituals in the country, millions of people have been exploited by this kind of exploitation. Many types of intellectual exploitation are clearly reflected in all areas of India's political, social, cultural and academic, and so forth.

Even today, the respect that authoritarianism, religious fundamentalism and monarchy are receiving in many countries of the world is the result of this hypnosis. In the Muslim-dominated countries of West Asia and Middle East Asia, the emergence of terrorist organizations such as an Islamic State and the gathering of adequate support, similar intellectual exploitation is a fierce example.

Spiritual creation of human

This world is highly diversified. From natural resources to human nature this variety is evident. In reality, this diversity creates beauty. In fact, we are all one in the eyes of God or Creator, but discrimination in practice remains. Probably this discrimination will continue to exist forever. If it is a universal belief that all the people of the world believe in the same type of world opinion, then it will be absolutely impossible. This can never happen, because the curiosity and diversity are the basis of human nature.

The same type of ritual practice or the same kind of lifestyle or ideology cannot be practiced all over the world. Neither this has ever happened, nor is there a possibility in the future. If ever this happen, so in practice this nature and its attraction will completely disappear, because diversity is the basis of human life and the basic attraction of this nature. Those who consider themselves as the best and want to impose it on others and look forward to creating a world based on one type of opinion, and for this, they don't even let go without walking in the path of violence and terrorism, they probably do not know the true aspect of nature and human nature. They do not even know that 'strange' is the original wall of life.

All the attraction and innovation of nature and the universe are embodied in this 'horizon'. This is the reason that individuals of different types of races are found in different regions of the world. There are different types of weather and climate created by nature. This diversity is the attraction of this universe. In fact, everything created by nature is beautiful. It will be said to be psychopath that we consider ourselves to be more beautiful and superior, and to undermine the other.

If we read all the scriptures of the world, even then it is possible that however, we do not have any knowledge of God or religion as well. It is also possible that we can talk about words and discourses of knowledge and spirituality all the time, even then, we cannot have any spiritual progress. Whether our intellect is most intensely, even among the scholars born around the world, but still they could not even recommend a slightest route to reach God. There is a clear experience of this world and the entire humanity that even after the highest intellectual education, there have been many gross non-religious, violent and intolerant people in the world society. Even today, the world is suffering from terrorism arising out of this kind of non-religious and intolerant movement. It is surprising that by condemning the killings of thousands of innocent civilians in different places around the world by terror incidents, they declare themselves as worshipers of God and want to create a highly unscientific and inhuman system based on a vote in the whole world. There is a need to give correct spiritual knowledge to such misguided people.

Dharyate Iti Dharma

'Dharyate Iti Dharma'

Means, which can be held, which can lead to development and protection, that is only Dharma. In this order it should be assumed that Dharma in Indian Consciousness is not limited to worship methods only. Followers of different religions and worship methods can also become part of Indian philosophy. Indeed, India is a liberal country and here, from ancient times, all kinds of sects, cult, worship practices and civilizations have been nurtured. This is the reason that in India Chaarvak, who was against the Vedas is being considered as a philosopher, and

Creation of New India

Mahatma Buddha, Mahavir Swami, Guru Nanak, Kabir and Satya Sai are considered as Godly form.

In fact, the help that gives us spiritual strength is the best one. After that comes, intellectual support and then physical help. By physical help only one cannot get rid of the world's sorrows. As long as human nature does not change, then these physical needs will remain unchanged and consequently the experience of distress will always be there. No amount of physical help can treat it completely. There is only one solution to that problem and it is to purify mankind. We see the inauspicious and tribulation that surrounds us, all of them have only one basic reason– Ignorance.

As long as man's character does not change, it will continue to cause all misery. Only through spiritual knowledge our endless grief, tension and misfortune can end forever. Therefore, to help a person spiritually, it is its biggest help. The person, who can give theological knowledge, is the greatest beneficiary of human society. Individuals who have given spiritual help to other humans are actually the most powerful and capable. The reason is that spirituality is the true basis of all acts from our lives. If a spiritually competent person wishes, then he can overcome all subjects. As long as there is no spiritual force in man, his physical needs cannot be satisfied as well.

If we make extensive study of the life, philosophy and character of the great personalities of the world, then it is clearly seen that sadness rather than happiness, and the poverty rather than the property is the only thing that have provided more education and inspiration to these great men. Similarly, the pains made them more determined and knowledgeable than praise. If a religion is to be useful for most people, then it should have the capacity to collect suitable material for people of different classes and where there is a lack of capacity, all sects there become a nation itself. A national expression which is found in Hinduism is definitely due to Spirituality in Hinduism. It is not possible to see such power in the definition of God, in any other religions and in any other religious texts of the world.

Unfortunately today's materialistic man has established relations with God and nature in accordance with religion, but in relation with God, man has given importance to the element of selfishness more than love. In human beings, today the desire to receive worldly things from God is high, because he feels that the real happiness of life is in these consumeristic substances. He keeps on trying himself for fulfilling worldly desires for a lifetime, and also asks for help from God. There are times when he get things beyond hope then he begin to feel the grace of God on himself. He gets serious about the worshipping of God and the element of love seems to be strong. It seems that religion has become a veil, but when its transient work does not work or he does not get the desired economic benefit, then immediately his love and devotion towards God reaches the lowest level and the business thinking of the transaction starts becoming effective. Attempts to establish a connection based on dealings with God are a symbol of the greatness of God and ignorance towards its qualities.

Liberation from chaos

Lord Buddha has said– 'The mind is everything. So whatever you want, it is possible it would happen like that way.' Due to weakness of our mind, we are actually defeated. If we were weakened and defeated, it would mean that we gave failures, an opportunity, to dominate our thoughts and we moved in the opposite direction from reality, in order to know ourselves. Success is rarely achieved by a weak mind. In his mind and heart, this thing has made up in his mind that he is incompetent. They do not have the ability to face difficulties, problems and crisis, and remove them. As such, even if the signs of success are visible even then they may not be acceptable and comprehensible to them. On the contrary, great disruption obstacles in front of those with strong morale also

   Creation of New India

become inferior. Because they have an optimistic view of solving all kinds of problems. Also because of their optimistic approach ultimately they are successful.

In Geeta too, one of the best ways to get rid of grief is described as Karma yoga. In Geeta, the human beings have been taught to be constantly engaged in karma. Of course, karma itself is a result in itself. In fact when karma is done without worrying about the result its efficiency also increases. In fact it is a psychology, which was explained in the Geeta prior to ages. The intent is clear that when we enjoy our work, then this happiness is a result in self. The quality of the result increases with pleasure from work. While working at the office, doing study, teaching, writing etc., doing farming or doing any kind of work, we can absorb all our consciousness. Whether he or she does not get proper remuneration, the progress of our activity is absolutely sure. We may be in conflict, but we will never feel the need to ask this question that what is sadness? Because sorrow will also get absorbed in the energy involved in doing 'karma'. We can live in a state of freedom from being in mourning.

O

7

Sacrifice makes the Country Strong

There is a need to make very intensive effort to eradicate inequality and hypocrisy from society. For this, new social renaissance and religious reform movements should be made. It is such a task, which can be accomplished only by the enterprise of society. To liberate social discrimination, it is necessary that we uproot those virtues, customs and unscientific beliefs from our personal and social life, which have caused great damage to India in the form of Indian society and a nation for thousands of years. Indian nationals must be excluded from their own contemplation and conduct as well as the subtler remnants of caste, communal, linguistic, ego. The source of the Hindu place of worship, the place of funeral and the source of water flow should be equally open to all Hindus; It is in fact the responsibility of every person in the society. Such programs should be organized in the name of the great men of various faiths, languages, provinces, castes of Hindus, and participation of all Hindus in festivals, such initiatives should be done in the immediate widespread society.

The lack of vision has never happened with us. On the basis of our eternal values, periods of individual and collective life-coherent thoughts have also been kept by many great men in front of society every time. Today's requirement is to bring such superior and ideal ideas into practice. The establishment of a consistent and ideal society will never be possible without the distinction between

'Kathni' and 'Karni'. The need to patiently build a collective enterprise on the basis of virtues in the society, awareness, integration, personal and national character, discipline etc is being felt today in India. If this could happen then it would certainly be possible to set a nation life ahead of all the challenges and crises to a balanced, happy, all-round, beautiful, global life.

In today's era, every human being suffers from ego and selfishness. Due to this ignorance, there has been a long gap between human and humanity. Human emotion are getting extinct. The existence of life values is becoming meaningless. Modern human has become so kind that he needs his own happiness, his fame and his own domination. Because of the ego, the attitude of the person becomes very limited, whereas there is a sense of warmth in the person with a generous vision. The basic formula of best practices is cordiality and tolerance. The sense of goodwill means– Expressing happiness by seeing the specialty of others, to promote the specialty of others and with intuitive expression it has to reach the public.

When the lamp of humanity extinguishes in the society, then darkness spreads everywhere. Due to the degradation of this humanity today, the world is suffering from many problems, injustice and violence. In an unmanned society, man does not have any knowledge of good and evil, duty-free, inattentive, purity-profane. Today, the whole world is troubled with unique reasons. In fact, there are pleasures in this world too and sadness too. The sensation of both of them is due to the existence of each other. The significance of the day is that the night comes and the importance of the night is that the day comes after it. The truth is that everyone wants to be happy, no one wants grief. This is the reason why the person searches for a way of redress, so that he can live happily, but the direction of his quest is wrong. He does not want to change himself. His desire always remains to see others' changing. It is clear that internal changes coming from within can give us a permanent solution to overcome problems and grief.

Nation demands devotion and sacrifice

In fact, by abusing the voluptuous culture of the West, we are sowing the seeds of destruction for ourselves. The consumerism created and circulated by the West is causing huge losses to Indian society, however, the whole of India is being entangled in its hypnosis without thinking of it. In fact, Western countries are getting direct economic benefits from consumerism and they are becoming prosperous. Since most of the products are manufactured and marketed by the Western countries, their citizens are increasingly becoming more prosperous and happy day by day. Nothing is achieved from countries such as India. This typhoon of consumerism has made us mentally, ideologically, socially and economically poor. We are getting poor like this, because of which we are not able to see our poverty.

The only consequence of this broad hypnosis of consumerism is that today Indian citizens do not have confidence in their culture, nor on their glorious history and performance. Today, Indians are disturbed by their own life values, and that is why even after many decades of independence, in India, the sense of– to live-to die, for national consciousness and the country has not been developed. The situation is that today, when an average Indian is criticized for Indian culture, values and national achievements, so he either takes silence or himself starts speaking the language of critics.

Originally Indian life philosophy is a living philosophy that is manifested by Gita. Mahatma Gandhi himself considered the work of Gita as the basis of Indian life philosophy. In his view, the Gita was not just a religious book. Unfortunately in India, for some reasons, some people are seen ignoring this symbol of national pride and contemplation. It is ironic that in the country where Gita's Karma yoga had originated, the same country has been acting, doing its work in just opposite way. This situation is not auspicious for the nation. In contrast, Europe, America, Israel and Australia appear on the peak on the global stage today, the reason is their citizens'

Karma yoga. Indian nationals also have to put themselves in the fire of Karma Yoga. Due to the state of impoverishment, today India is lacking in every field on the global stage. It can be changed.

Glorification of slavery

This is the misfortune of India that after achieving independence, no effort was made to awaken national consciousness and glory in the country. There are several points on which we should have worked as an independent nation. Even today, symbols of slavery everywhere are being glorified in every corner of the country. Certainly this is happening because of our ignorance. Even today, various cities, metros and even in the capital of the country, names of various monuments, roads, routes, buildings and public places are in the name of such persons who were purely anti-India by their consciousness and Karma. It is a matter of 'shame' that even after six decades of independence, the sense of our consciousness and national identity has not been awakened.

If the patriots such as Bhagat Singh, Lala Lajpat Rai, Madan Mohan Malaviya, Sardar Patel, Dr. Hedgewar, Subhash Chandra Bose and Dr. Ambedkar were alive today, then surely they would not let the country remain as unconscious and unmanifest. After the country's independence, the ruling governments in the country separated themselves from the national consciousness and pride due to their vested interests and this led to the decline of the country intellectually and mentally. By the influence of Western economists, the governments of the country assumed only physical development as the last index of development that is why the development of the country in independent India has remained confined to development in the field of technical and consumer goods only.

India's development journey in independent India started under the leadership of Jawaharlal Nehru. Nehru was essentially influenced by Western education and mentality and that is why he tried to impose the same rationality gained from the West on India.

In his long tenure as Prime Minister of the country, there had been no serious effort done to awaken and strengthen the consciousness of the country in the right way. His focus was concentrated on the country's foreign policy, industrial development and administration. Without denying his contribution, it can be said that he did not utilize his strong political position to make India as a strong and capable nation.

India is a huge country of 125 crore citizens. Unfortunately, in an independent India, no effort has been made to properly cognize, educate and train citizens about their responsibilities towards the nation. Most Indian citizens do not contemplate about the nation in their daily lives. If the citizen contemplates about the nation before doing any small or big task, he will surely be able to realize the quality of the work done by him. It is also surprising that there are many such tasks which citizens should do themselves, but they look helplessly towards the government and administration for those tasks. After all why? Many small tasks can be done by the citizens with collective participation. This will not only make citizens conscious and active at the individual level, but the society and the nation will also have widespread benefits.

Dutiful citizens can build a healthy and prosperous society and nation. After all, why have we become so dependent on the government and the planning system that we cannot discharge our responsibilities by following civil right ourselves? This tendency is not good that we ourselves do not fulfill any kind of responsibility and keep blaming others at all times. We should also see what are we doing on serious issues related to the country and what contribution and commitment do we have for the society and the nation?

Following lewd culture

Change is the law of life. Everyone knows this thing, but the change that is taking place at this time has developed distortion. The incidents happening in society are compelling us to think that finally where is this leading us? Today often, there is talk of change, but social values are sidelined.

Our families and educational institutions are responsible for establishing social values. Earlier, people had faith in cultural beliefs, but gradually the belief is continuously decreasing. The culture of the West is being imitated without thinking. Growing up of Western culture in the society and making distance from its culture is also pushing the society in the wrong direction. It is a matter of surprise that Western countries love their civilization, culture and traditions more and have a close engagement with them. In fact, the Western countries are spraying their 'cultural garbage' in countries like India because of their policies for gaining economic benefits. Unfortunately, by adopting this 'garbage', a vast majority of Indians with inferiority complex feel proud of themselves.

Due to the influence of the 'cultural waste' of the West, there is a continuous decrease in traditional knowledge and life values in Indian homes. Social values through TV and Internet are being damaged very rapidly. Although modern tools related to information and technology are created in terms of creative use, but they are misused on a widespread scale. The number of people in the world of negative tendencies is increasing and they learn to exploit the creative products and tools which has been created for useful purposes. Human nature is often more inclined towards negative actions in place of constructive objects. This human trend is constantly sustained and developed by anti-social people.

TV and Internet can be the best medium of knowledge, science and research, but their creative use in India is very less. In India, programs related to science, research and investigation are not shown much on TV, whereas in the Western world there is a lot of such creative programs and research-based specialist channels. In India, we prefer only shallow entertainment, song, music, comedy and family drama, rather than knowledge, science and research based programs.

It is clear that 'communication revolution' has already arrived in India, but India still remains away from the 'information revolution'. From morning to evening, the Indian channels continue to show sloppy and extravagant serials and programs. Seeing these programs, Indian society don't get anything. On one hand, time is being wasted; on the other hand the intellectual consciousness of the citizens is eroded. It is clear that whatever is going wrong in Indian society, we cannot just impose blame on the Western countries. Why don't we imitate their good things? If Indian values are going down steadily from the social life, then Indian citizens themselves are more responsible for this.

Today, the social values are breaking down. Those educational institutions, who used to go to increase the socialization process in the country, and where lessons were taught about the formation of family, relationships, social values, nationality and national character, the institute is now only for acquiring job, completing technical curriculum by any means. Today, no one is ready to teach moral values. Our fore-fathers were more cautious about ethical values. The elderly in the homes, used to try to awaken the moral values of children from infancy, but today there is no one to follow the teachings of the elderly.

Instead of learning from the elderly people, they have been treated as a useless and burden from society. Earlier distant relationships also had great importance in the life and social life of the person. Today, not only distant relationships, but their importance is also being diminished. Children living in cities today do not know the meaning of these relationships. Apart from parents, they have no information about a large family and society. When this child goes to the village or the countryside, then he feels very awkward.

It seems that these children either are roaming abroad or have come from abroad, and they have no information about any of the Indian society. This pretence and hypocrisy, in the name of development, is creating many types of classes in India. This has led to a severe imbalance and inequality in the country.

Not materiality, excellence is important

The tragedy of the modern generation is that the target of their life is only to achieve economic prosperity. The discussion of religion, spirituality and ethics for the modern generation has ceased to be a topic of interest. Due to increasing mental stress, depression and unbelief in society, life values are getting eroded very fast. Apart from this, obstacles are also being created in social and family configuration. Looking at the demand of time, we must develop morality by purification conduct. The initial philosophy of Lord Mahavira was also contained in the Moral Code of Ethics, that is valuable for every one. In fact, following the values of life and ethical conduct is a symbol of true 'religion'.

The holes of unethical conduct can be blocked only by giving morality in the form of resistive power. Evil and sin deeds can be discouraged only by purification of thoughts in person, society and nation. The second name of the purity of ethics is only 'religion'.

By looking at different types of life styles around us we try to imitate them. We want to imitate the kind of food high class people eat, how to get up or sit and behave like them etc. in the society. Most of the time while imitating, we also do not even think that whether these behaviors are favorable to our way of life or not. To follow that action or behavior it is also essential to be friendly to them.

Due to different life styles and cultural exchanges all over the world through the Internet today Western countries have been competing to imitate the behaviors and practices without knowing it. Drugs and adultery are being fashioned in our country even today by the blindness of the West. India is also victims of this kind of cultural and ideological assault. This situation is not auspicious and we should be reflective of our own atmosphere, environment and values, in order to develop ourselves. Only copying someone will not increase our pride. By imitating we will be preoccupied with ideological and mental slavery.

Physical and consumeristic objects and temporal property also have their own importance, but to the extent that, their attainment and achievement did not affect human excellence. From the point where the physical virtues and the ego of the temporal properties begin to affect excellence, from there they become utterly abandoned. In fact, each person's capacity is fulfilled. There is a store of abilities in it. When the Creator created the human race, then first he would have kept his difficulties in mind and then included the extraordinary capabilities in man to face them, but today's human has become misguided. He is not able to see his abilities and talents. This is the reason why most of the people today are adopting 'shortcuts' for success. Today, man is not hesitant to compromise with the values of life to achieve success. It is true that we are living in a meaningful era where economic development is considered as an alternative to overall development. The result is also in front of us. From morning to evening most of the citizens continue to discuss only about financial issues. Society and nation are not anywhere in their priority list. The heartbeat of these types of people increases and decreases with the unimaginable ups and downs of Sensex.

O

8

Building on a Weak Foundation

Indian social values are speedily being eroded. As a result of this, different types of criminal incidents continue to appear. Some time ago, there was a news from Gautam Buddha Nagar of Uttar Pradesh that the alchohol addict husband put his wife at stake in gambling. This type of news tells the story of declining Indian social values. This type of news really indicates that in the changing modern lifestyle, the greed has also increased in people. Greed makes the person blind and he forgets what is right and what is wrong?

The trend of ATM Father culture is growing rapidly in the society. It will often be seen that the father is having fun with his acquaintances and their children are enjoying at the same place in their group. Parents have given ATM cards for money to their children, but they are not aware of the knowledge of good and evil. Parents' liability is not completed by giving only money to the children. In fact, in lieu of not properly discharging your responsibilities, it is the bribe given by parents only to their kids. It seems that corruption and bribe termite has littered the Indian consciousness and life values, and its effect can be seen everywhere in India's socio-cultural-family-administrative-political life.

When the foundation is weak, then the building can't be expected to be strong. After all, what are we giving to children? For this, the elderly will also have to think. Growing communication gap with children is also dangerous. Parents give their responsibility to others. This also causes criminal offences with children. The cases of sexual assault have also increased by the relatives on very young children. This is happening excessively in the middle class family, where people close to the family are involved, but due to so-called prestige and the pressure of the relationship, most of the cases are dubbed. Such incidents have a bad effect on the lives of children and they get stressed and face many mental disorders. Loneliness of people and Social Media are mostly responsible for ending our social fabrication. Materialism, consumerism and widening social gaps are more responsible for this.

In cosmopolitan civilization, today's trend of single-family is becoming very high. It has many social, economic and psychological reasons. The problem is that there are no grandparents, uncles who have social control over children in single families. The current single family has been confined to the husband-wife and children only. Parents are working and children are alone at home. There is no one to teach them the moral values. Every man is busy in his world. He does not get any meaning because of the troubles of others, nor does he has any time for it.

In the olden times, elderly people of the house used to be conscious and alert about the right and wrong of the children. Elders always educate human relationships, connection and life values. In today's society, respect for humility and elders is continuously diminishing. So far, the culture of foreign invasions has been considered responsible for devaluation of social values. But today, during the period of economic liberalization, globalization, the explosion of openness in information has shaken the social beliefs. The effect of imitation, and copy of Western culture, from the Internet to the movies, is clearly been seen in society. Due to the public demonstration of Western culture, due to the public display of sexual desires, in the media, many types of contaminated traits have started to emerge in the society. This thinking considers the

                                    Creation of New India

woman as merely an object of enjoyment and keeps aside the relations. Earlier, the tradition of rural culture and joint families provided protection to women, but today all the flaws of single families have started to emerge.

Children are also suffering due to their working parents. Parents involved in making money to compete are losing their children's faith rapidly. Various changes have come in modern Indian society. In the cities, there is a trend of single families. Due to the efforts of women empowerment, they are also coming out in large number for work. In such a situation, there has been a great change in traditional Indian lifestyle. Now the person is deprived from all the benefits and facilities of joint families. In the cities, working couples put more time in office and also have to suffer traffic congestion after office hours. The result is that they can't get any time for personal relationships, family and their social concerns. Because of this, social turmoil, and love & affection in personal relations are rapidly getting over.

Old social and family relationships are almost finished off. In the metros, 'flat culture' has promoted the culture of Single family in place of the Joint family. People in the Joint family and traditional social system were most afraid of public shame, but now that fear is ending. Today both husband and wife are working. Due to the pressure of job and work, they can't spend much time with the children. In this way, children are getting away from love and affection.

Due to the rapid decline in social and moral values, the impact is visible everywhere in the society. Indian family and relatives also could not save themselves from this fall. In India, relationships like maternal uncle, paternal uncle had always been of great importance, but now these relationships are getting tainted. Such immoral acts shock us. Increasing drug abuse in society is also one of the major reasons in making the relationships stain. A person having addiction of alcohol or any other intoxicants is more susceptible to such type of immoral activity. Unfortunately, in Indian society, the intoxication is continuously getting approval and support on a large scale. Young people in large number are becoming entangled in the dilemma of becoming 'fashionable'. This leads to crime and immorality in the society.

Marriage institution becomes weak

Today Indian youth is avoiding or getting away from marriage or any kind of relationship. Earlier, when their studies were completed and they got jobs then the preparation of boys' wedding used to start, now such things are not seen in our society. Even after the age of 35-36, the tendency of avoiding any relationship is termed as Committed Phobia by the psychiatrist. According to a survey conducted in India, 15 percent of the youth living in Indian cities suffer from this Committed Phobia. Indian urban youth are often afraid of bonding in any kind of relationship or even those who have been tied up, want to become free from that bond. Due to the fear of their freedom loss, the youth don't want to stay in any bond. Instead of getting bind in the social circle, they want to live life independently.

Today, the fact is that, in India, the large number of youth of the country is still afraid of marriages, even after getting job or aging. In many places, such youths are being treated with psycho therapy. There is no synergy in mutual thoughts, lack of understanding, lack of patience and tolerance, increased irritability, economic independence, increasing dependency on electronic gadgets and experiences of fear of past marital relationships in relations and family, are the main reasons for Committed Phobia. Due to fear of accountability and increased responsibilities in connection with relationships also leading towards Committed Phobia. To avoid Committed Phobia, psychiatrists are advising people to go for Psycho therapy. By doing counselling, they are finding the reasons and trying to reduce it accordingly.

 Creation of New India

The growing world of electronic gadgets and the growing trend of the 'single family' has increased the number of youth in the city who do not take any relationship seriously. Psychologists are indicating that the modern youth generation can't stay in relationships with anyone for a long time.

Along with economical, technological and scientific development in India, social and family values have undergone rapid changes in the past decades. Different types of established traditions and institutions are becoming weak today. Due to not being able to keep pace with the modern times, many good traditions and life values are becoming endangered by society. Marriage institutions are also affected by these changes. As a result of economic reforms, academic development and the increasing trend of single families, there is no such sacred belief in marriage among the youth, such as in the past. This has resulted in manifold incidents of marriage dissection and family segregation in society.

In this context, the young people have got acceptance of new ideas, which give greater importance to personal interest and personal freedom, in place of abandonment and reciprocal responsibility. It is also a plea of the younger generation that for the pleasure and contentment you accept marriage bond, on the basis of mutual understanding, if you make a composite combination, if it is finished, then it is better to separate. Sociologists say that there are so many pairs, among whom the love has dried up, but they are no different and pretend to be a happy couple in front of people, because society looks at divorce with weird eyes.

People have started understanding that the exploitation of the seven births was being exploited by the people. The number of people considering the option of divorce to get out of such troublesome bondage is now on in India too. More than 43 thousand divorces have been officially happened in India in 2014, 60 percent of which were on mutual agreement. It is clear that the separation of marriages and relations, this generation of Indian is thinking with a new perspective.

There is a need to see divorce by connecting with Indian spirituality and philosophy. This should not be seen in connection with the traditional ritualistic thinking. World over in many religions and sects any bond has been considered as a hindrance in the progress of any individual. To get freedom from a bond is the only salvation. The saint who is called the bond of illusion, what is this? It is our emotional dependence on other people. When this dependency is over, then we become free. Become independent. Marriage is also a kind of dependency. If it becomes completely bound, then divorce leads to liberation. There is a need to adopt a new progressive approach to the institution of marriage. Cerebralistic thinking has enhanced the inertia of Indian society and has led to frustration in personal life. The country is not getting the right benefit of talented human resources.

Hard to follow ideals

Such a person who does not leave his life principles, values, faith and resolutions despite any of the circumstances does not allow to grow bad character, defects, and other ill things within, that personality is really praise worthy and eligible for emulation. It is as easy to sell for the vested interests in this world, it is equally difficult to stay on the narrow paths of ideals and life values. The path of morality and significance is rather tough, whereas the path of immorality and depreciation is quite smooth.

Indian philosophy inspires tolerance. Indian intellectuals and spiritualists have gladly accepted condemnation and criticism. In the context of condemnation and criticism, the Indian experience tells that in the Indian social life, often the purpose of slander is not to improve but failure is more. His work by doing evil of someone to calm the spirit of God's will, frustration and retribution. Positive thinking in terms of condemnation is to find good for yourself.

Kabirdas also thanked the slanderer who criticized him a lot. In this way he got free from bad qualities. Condemnation pointing towards the faults and errors, inspires them to overcome. In place of unheeding, listening to his condemnation should be considered carefully. If there is any essence in that condemnation, then it is appropriate to adopt it and improve it. If condemnation is immaterial, then there is no need to worry about it. Even if the condemnation is not immaterial, it also gives an opportunity, an opportunity to see and self-assess.

We are usually surrounded by many problems in our lives. To get rid of these problems, we use to look for smaller paths. Because of being ignorant and ignorance ofwork we don't entrust to take the responsibility of building our destiny on our own shoulders and entrust them to the hands of such persons whose own merit and wisdom are questionable. Often we are rescued by those who are themselves involved in their own problems. One poet has said, "Had hold the hand of that person, who himself needed a help." That is why it is said that whenever you find yourself in a state of crisis, you should go in the shelter of the scriptures. Actually our life is a kind of Mahabharata and all of us are like Abhimanyu, who can enter in the maze of difficulties, but does not know how to come out of it. Positive thinking, disciplined behavior and Karma yoga can only take us out of this maze.

Imitation needs intelligence

Indian culture is unique in its own way. After all, why are we destroying our attribute by merely copying the West? Discarding the originality, today Indian society is just carrying the blame of a imitator. When other countries of the world can take pride in their culture, language and living, then why can't Indians do this? We are becoming imitator in such a way that we have squeezed and sidelined the proper rituals from our good and scientific perspective and have adopted the unscientific symbols of Western culture without thinking.

Due to being deprived of deprivation, we have rejected many of the best Indian traditions without considering it. There are many such Indian traditions, manners and behaviors, which are far more scientific and rational. As such, in the Indian tradition, we greet each other by saying Namaskar, whereas on the contrary, in the Western countries, they follow 'hand shake'. The Indian traditions prove far more authentic and useful on many medical, scientific and human health related matters. If seen, there is no transition in the Indian tradition of Namaskar, but there is only contact. Our Namaskar is far more scientific, clean and dignified. Similarly, in Europe people make a bouquet of flowers and give it in hand. Flowers are tied in bouquets. We have the tradition of giving garlands, in which different kind of flowers are stitched together. Each flower is free from other. While the transit is reflected in the bouquet, the Indian garland has a sense of contact. Garland is a symbol of Indian civilization, while bouquet is a symbol of Western culture. This fact may seem small, but there is also a clear philosophy, thinking and psychology behind this.

The main thing in Indian culture is that the emphasis is not on touching the body. If there is any recognition of touch in Indian philosophy, consultation and practice, that is for doing service. These rules and traditions associated with daily life can also be linked with the intensification of issue of cleanliness and health in India. It is obvious that we should not abandon our best traditions, which are definitely much healthier as per scientific point of view also.

We must always remember the basic elements of our civilization and culture and and shouldn't follow others' blindly. The real ideal for Indian citizens can be the person, who have sacrificed everything for this nation and society. Most of the world's greatest men are born in India. Indian land has been the work place of many great workers such as Rama, Krishna, Bhishma, Buddha, Mahavir Swami, Nanak, Kabir, Raidas. Indian culture is not based on enjoyment and pleasures but based on real knowledge and life values. This is only the real truth of life.

We will not be left anywhere in imitating Western consumerism. India's uniqueness is lying in its original culture and ideology. Our ideal can only be a Karmayogi born on our land. The shallow person engaged in the enjoyment of the Western land can't think of Indian society to be the ideal. If this happened, then the social structure in India and the fundamental Indian philosophy will be affected.

Show-Off

Unnecessarily displaying of power, strength and level, in India, is becoming a permanent trend among most citizens. This kind of behavior is not appreciable. Misuse of power and strength increases chaos and immorality in society. This kind of behavior increases the differences and inequality among civilian citizens. Society and nation with distinction and inequality can never get respect. The position and the power given by it must be in order to really get motivated towards duty, but often the high-ranking people do not even bother to foment with the dignity of the nation in their false lust to increase their dignity. This situation is extremely pathetic and it should be changed immediately.

The incidents of disrespectful behavior with national symbols are often seen to be exposed. Indian national symbols and emblem should be a symbol of respect and dignity for every citizen. In the developed nations of the West, citizen does not hesitate to put his life at stake to protect the value of national symbols. Indian citizens should also develop similar feelings in themselves.

The pillar that Ashoka made in Sarnath, its top portion is called Singh Chaturmukh. In this statue, four lions are standing back to back of each other. The Ashoka pillar is still located in its original place, but its head is kept in the Museum of Sarnath. This Lion Chaturmukha pillar top has been acknowledged as the National symbol of India. India adopted this symbol on January 26, 1950. In India, clear written rules and laws have been made for all national emblems and national symbols such as national flag ie Tricolor, National anthem-Jana Gana Mana, National song-Vande Mataram, animal-tiger, aquatic animal-ganga dolphin, bird-peacock, flower-lotus, tree-banyan, fruit-mango, sports-hockey and *panchag-saka-samvat* etc. These laws and regulations must be followed. It is the duty of every citizen to respect these symbols for nation's pride.

It is often seen that our obligation to teach others is to teach more and it is rare for us to drop in. The cars running on the roads are full of red and blue top lights. People play hooters and don't follow traffic rules. A large no. of vehicles pertaining to the MPs, legislators, journalists etc. are running on the road bearing their name plates. All this is being done only because they could show themselves superior to other citizens. In violation of rules and regulations in India, it has become a sign of reputation for some people. Unfortunately, this type of behavior is done by those people, who are responsible for running the law and order.

There are many such citizens who follow the rules very well when they go out of the country but returning back to India they start doing the same kind of indisciplined and indecent behavior. This is an ugly face of our civilized society. We feel proud in breaking the system. People may have acquired technical and bookish knowledge today, but moral education is still lacks. Rules and laws are made to build a well-organized society. If every citizen has a respect for these laws and rules, then a better and well-structured system can be built. In the same way as children are taught to respect the elders, similarly, the teachings of the symbols of the nation and the teachings to follow the rules should also be given from their childhood.

 Creation of New India

Unnecessary fights

Indian citizens are becoming intolerant with different kinds of chaos and anarchy. This has become clear in many surveys and research. You go to any public place in India or on the road, you will be able to see people fighting for any unproductive or very useless things. People in the Indian society tend to quarrel for very silly issues and just waste their precious time. Indeed, unnecessary anger and irritability have become part of the mentality and behavior of Indian citizens today. There is no such dispute among the citizens on unnecessary things in developed countries, the kind of environment that is seen everywhere in India. This thing seems to be very small, but defines the whole character of a nation. A country will be exactly the same, as per its citizens' conduct, mindset and behaviour.

In terms of Indian conduct and behavior, it can be said that People in India speak much and listen very less. This is the reason that there is no sensitive discussion on serious issues in society. In fact, the person should listen more and speak less. This will not only save the energy, but also increases the ability to think and understand the person. When a decision is taken after listening and understanding the person speaking in front, then the decision be more logical and practical. One could be save from unnecessary stress, struggle and anger, which can be avoided by this habit. The topic on which the person has spoken and the circumstances under which the incident happened, should be evaluated. It's going to save you from unnecessary anger and then atonement.

In many Indian places of contemplation and philosophy, it has been said that the main enemy of man is anger. If it remains in the body only, then it destroys the whole body. The same thing has been clarified in relation to anger in the Gita, and it has been said that anger generates idiocy and due to this idiocy, 'memory gets misplaced'. Wisdom is destroyed by 'memory loss' and when the wisdom is destroyed, the person himself gets destroyed. If we conquer work, temptation, greed before winning the anger, then tension will go away. As soon as it goes away, we will become contented and will be saved from anger when it comes to satisfaction. To avoid stress we should take shelter in Yoga. It keeps us away from the evils of life. In the stressful environment of modern life, it is natural to have disorder in body and meditation. Disorders such as sex, anger, fear and suspicion prevents life from being balanced. Conscious citizens should not allow these disorders to come into their lives and they must constantly strive to give meaning to their life.

It is usually seen that behavioral changes are also shown in India due to socio-economic reasons. There is no doubt that all of us Indians today suffer from too much ego, tension and anger. On small issues, conflicts of ego in the country cause conflicts and tensions. This kind of behavior and psychology is not auspicious as a person and nation. It is important to control anger. It can be avoided from the fights of futility and we can put our precious time in more creative work.

Freedom of expression

The freedom of expression has been given constitutional recognition in the country, but it is often seen that under its clutches, chaotic elements produce a non-essential environment. This makes the nation's image blurred. Recently, the educated youth of the country have wasted their energy on many unproductive issues. This country saw how thousands of young people of the country came on the streets to fight for that unproductive issue, which would only lead to the loss of national energy. It would have been better if the energetic Indian youth would come to the streets to fight for national problems, instead of Kiss of Love, to solve national problems. If this were the case, then surely the hope of resolving the many national problems of the country is sure.

It needs to be understood that in this context, for the organizers and supporters of Kiss of Love, whatever is justified, it can be unlimited and unfair for all other people. Of course, freedom of

                                    Creation of New India

expression does not guarantee that you have a feeling of ideological or cultural violence towards another citizen. It is also not necessary that whatever behavior or conduct is not objectionable in the eyes of the law, it should also be accepted by the society as well. In terms of law, any two adult individuals can have sexual relations with mutual consent, but it is not necessary that the society should also give its consent.

In the eyes of society, some restrictions are necessary, so that social structure and its fabrication shouldn't be destructed. Not every practice can be seen strictly as per the law.

Although, there is no written constitution or law for family members in a house, nevertheless, members of the family are being taught lessons of conduct. If a younger member in a family disrespects elders, it does not make a crime in a legal sense, but it is unacceptable as per life values and rituals. No society can survive without such kind of cultures and values. As Live-in Relationship can be valid in terms of law, but a major part of the society don't accept. Many things are not a crime in terms of law, but they can prove to be fatal to social balance and configuration of life values.

In terms of law, any two adult individuals can have sexual relations with mutual consent, but in order to maintain the social structure, a number of boundaries have been set in this regard. Due to these limitations institutions such as society and family could have survived all over the world so far. Undoubtedly, without any discipline and well cultured social and moral values, a healthy and cultured society can't be established. Not everything should be treated according to law, but it should be done on the basis of social traditions and values, only then a healthy and balanced society will be established.

It is true that social beliefs gradually changes. It might be that after a decade or two, there would be such situation in India that nobody will bother about kissing or embracing youth in the public places, but till such a situation does not come, at least efforts should be made that this situation should not exist. Most Indian citizens have faith in ancient Indian culture, family and marriage institutions and life values. No one could ever be allowed to hurt that faith.

Cheap popularity

In Delhi, Kiss of Love was organized on the initiative of some students of Jawaharlal Nehru University. It should be a serious concern today that why has the well reputed Indian university become a place of shallow idea and cheap popularity? Many such universities and colleges of India deliberately do so much in the passion of proving themselves progressive and fashionable, which can't be praiseworthy or justified in any way. Regular programs for beef intake and intense desire for virginity are organized in many colleges. Some colleges also struggle to celebrate Mahishasur's birthday.

It is not understandable that what is ultimately going to be achieved by organizing such kind of illogical and indecent kind of things to some Indian students? In many colleges, the programs to be held regularly in the student festivals are severely obnoxious and objectionable. Standing on stage, using obscene conversations and slang language and abusive words is becoming a 'style statement' in the college. This kind of behavior is becoming a necessary condition for being progressive and minded. Some of today's youths seem to be very impressed with the 'AIB Roast' slut and duplicate programs. The language seems 'cool' to them. There is a need to think very seriously on this issue whether our educational centers are becoming the place of anti-social or anti-national activities under the guise of western culture and the left. This can also be possible because India is having liberal democratic system, where all types of anti-social and anti-national activities are accepted with great ease. This trend is fatal and destructive. In the near future, as a society and a nation, India may have to pay a huge price.

O

　　　　　　　　　　　　　　Creation of New India

9
Hypocrisy Free India

In India, the Religion has always been considered synonym of justice. There has been continuous confusion about the interpretation of the word of religion at the global level. Instead of confronting this delusion we ourselves have become a victim of confusion. In fact, why it happened, because our education and philosophy have been stuck worthlessly in terms of explanations given by the West. In our independent India, our education system is the imitation of the West and in this context Indian philosophy and spirit has been rejected. This is the reason that there is a sense of suspicion and ambiguity about the true meaning of religion in the country.

Religion is indeed an eternal element. For Indians, religion is a synonym of truth and justice. Today, the number of such people is increasing, who only wants to live at the level of body, mind and wisdom. Religion is such an experience, which itself has to be acquired. This is not just a philosophical hypothesis, but a rationality. The real power of religion is only possible through work. If religion has not been molded into action, then it will prove to be only a hypocrisy.

Unfortunately today, in the discussion of religion, humans often fall on the back foot and the rituals of worthless get the importance in their place. Along with that, all the selfishness has also become very prominent, which are associated with worship sites and deities. This demerit is seen everywhere in temples, mosques, churches etc. It is also true that with the increasing number of places of worship in the country, the average Indian is becoming more narrow minded and intolerant.

Today's man does not seek religion with him, but he wanders out in search of it, whereas religion is concerned only with the inner conscience of the person. In this context, it seems that the complete human being is yet to be born. It should be clear that religion is related to the very primary level of worship, recitation, chanting, and without it the person can also be available to Bodhatwa and religiousness.

Indeed, man has to constantly move forward in search of the truth. Dharmachakra is a symbol of this deep search of truth. In fact, for the complete development of the human being, it is not possible to think of a better concept than Dharmachakra, that is why the country's constitution makers, immediately after independence kept a proclamation for the Indian Parliament-Dharmachakrapravaratna. This word has been written in the golden letters on the seat of the speaker of the country's parliament. It is unfortunate that so far the political parties of the country and the representatives who sit in the House are fail to understand and inspire with this face. In fact, there should be vivid interpretation and continuous discussion of this social proclamation of the Indian parliament in the nation.

Damage to national pride

'Yatra Dharmo Haadharmen Satyam Yatraamritej che,
Hanyate Prekshmaadaanaam Hataastatra Sashasadah.'

That is, in the meeting, where in the presence of the assembly members the religion is defeated by lawlessness and truth is hurt by falsehood, there all the members or state representatives who endorse that sin are eventually finished.

In fact, when by any means or by power, injustice in any form is directly or indirectly and if support is provided, then the society is born with a wide range of exploitation. It is the obligation of

Creation of New India

any country's judicial system to end such exploitation at every level. Exploitation is a mental illness that can occur at any level of person, institution or organization. Exploitation can't be excused in any of its form. It must be completely eliminated from India because it is not accepted on behalf of the person and the society, nor should it be done.

Communalism is actually the result of the deviation of common divinity towards this divided consciousness and national interest. The existence of tolerance and generosity with communalism is impossible. In fact, religion can never be intolerant or communal in its totality. People who see religion in divided form are having narrow thinking and this gives rise to communalism. For world peace, we must abandon communalism. Today, the necessity is that all India must unite and have the courage to speak openly and stand up against communalism. In reality, the difference between religion and religiousness must be understood. Due to misunderstanding about this, our national pride is being damaged today and contempt of national identity is happening. In our six decades of Independent India, even if thousands of kilometers of roads, big industries, foreign capital investment and large scale production plants and factories are established in the country, but mentally this country is till dwarf. In the 21st century, India have the challenge of leaving this dwarfism and show its natural and gigantic form to the world.

It is often said that the general mindset of Indian priests is based on selfishness. They have started trading of the religion and God-Goddesses. They have become egoistic rather providing service to the people. Sometimes the ego increases so high that they do not even care to violate the general etiquette. It is a matter of concern that how such a person will behave well for the society and the nation, because they neither worry about humanity nor the nation itself. The truth is that their level of knowledge is also very limited. He has neither studied Indian philosophy nor superior scriptures and literature. Their whole focus is limited to rituals and processes.

This is also a topic of thinking and research after all, how do these priests become financially capable within a very short time? The truth is that 'spirituality' is not a matter of any kind of scholarship. Spiritual meditation is not dependent on priests and religious leaders. Any person is completely independent of doing the best spiritual meditation, that's why in every age, Mahavira, Buddha, Nanak, Kabir, Dadu, Raidas like the thinkers have always been born.

The relation of spiritual contemplation is never related to the dynasty. The best qualities have to be earned through your talent and hard work. Excellent quality and divine thinking can't be inherited by any person naturally, rather they have to earn this by putting efforts by themselves. The son of a player will not be able to become an efficient player because his father was a skilled player, but he must earn this skill himself. The country has to free itself from the tide of Exorcism, Amulets, Garlands. There is no other option except this. The country has to be molded into the thinking of a modern, scientific, progressive and integrated humanism.

Many routes, one target

Various concepts of 'fate' and 'adorable' are prevalent in different cultures and societies. All the religions, societies and cultures have recognized any almighty, adorable or power. Based on these assumptions, some principles, life-style, traditions and sanskars have been developed so as to create an organized and strong social structure.

God is also in different forms according to the times of the country. There are many ghats in a large pond, having the same water on every ghat. It's not a good thing to argue on the issue of water. All religions act as a means of bringing human beings to the same ghat. With the help of any one of the ghats, with passion and reverence, we can get into the other lake.

                                    Creation of New India

There is no point in saying about religion's superiority. Due to ignorance, one considers the other as inferior to one's religion. This kind of ignorance leads to unnecessary stress and chaos in society. When the knowledge of reality comes, then this discord also becomes calm. It is often seen that there is no moss in large ponds and clean water. On the contrary, moss is produced in small ponds and dirty water. It is clear that in the communities and societies, people work purely, generously, and selflessly in the work of humanity, even among them many corrupt things like 'Kai' (moss) does not flourish.

Just as nature and the sky can't be divided, so God can't be seen even by dividing the religions and sects. Actually all the religions practiced in the world are equal and mutually beneficial. There is no conflict among them, but they all have the same goal– the welfare of humans only. It is clear that peace cannot be established in human society at large scale without taking into account the distinct human welfare and meaning of religion.

When will the creed end

"O majestic sadness,
the blood of the joy of young spring is felt on your hands."

– Pankaj Singh

A major tension in Hindu society has arisen due to social evils. Many practices are running in such a trend that is demanding to spend a lot of money. A middle-class person can honestly earn as much as possible, in which his family can live in some way. It is not possible for ordinary people to go for long-term savings during the inflation period. The prevalent practices of the society, superstitious and antiquated traditions make the common man a lot of money and time wastage. Indian citizens have not been able to get rid of these crimes yet. Numerous rural and poor citizens still lose their entire lives in fulfilling many unscientific rites and rituals. Despite all this, there is no salvation for them, but they have more economic, mental and social decline.

For the person trapped in many economic compulsions, the prevalent charities and superstitions in society are a total of suicidal tendencies. Crores of poor and distressed people have to find a way to get rid of these traps of hanging. Despite all this, our mental impairment does not allow us to think that, are these social evils really logical and in any way necessary for life? Indian society must now test the logic of these rituals– customs from a scientific perspective.

Dowry, the problem of the marriage of the educated girl, the perverted nature of the caste system, the discrimination of the sub-castes, the discrimination of male and female, the veil system in rural areas, obscenity, child marriage, expensive marriage, education, business, death feasts, huge investment in ornaments, concocted trap of ghosts and spirit, sorcery, superstitions, population growth, feticide etc. are making the society hollow. India has been the slave of these dogmas for thousands of years. Because of these very unscientific beliefs, Indian society has become a characteristic of egoism. Due to these fabricated practices, the Indian society has not been able to advance with self-respect by becoming self-reliant. The trend of such stereotypes should be declared as 'anti-nationalism' and should be abolished by creating stringent laws and eliminating them.

○

 Creation of New India

10

Colonial Hypnosis

The Constitution of India is the world's most elaborated constitution, yet this constitution is unable to discipline India's undemocratic society. Many times the question arises that whether the Indian society's mindset is completely undemocratic? There are many such developed countries in the world where there is no written constitution of any kind, as in the UK. Similarly, there are many other nations, having very briefly written constitution, such as America. Even after having an unwritten and very briefed constitution, there is a better law and order and 'rule of law' better than ours. Indeed, in countries like America and Britain, their healthy democratic traditions keep them disciplined in this way.

Unfortunately, in India, there is a lacking of perpetual and continuous civil liability perception of such healthy democratic traditions and nation. In simple sense, the conventions are known as traditions in India. For a long time, the majority of traditions or customs in India are also prevalent, they are really negative and they have been more harmful to the nation and the society till now. India has not been so mature enough in the form of a nation, that in its own way pretentious, orthodox, unscientific and harmful practices for society and nation and learn to distinguish between healthy and democratic traditions.

In fact, traditions develop according to the need in society, whereas convergence is often imposed on a relatively uneducated or minority society, by a resource-rich and prosperous society. With its healthy and rational traditions, nations such as Great Britain and America, which have been established as a mature democratic society, India is still a 'undemocratic' and 'unscientific' society in dealing with its narrow beliefs. We have so far been unable to establish a rational democratic society. In India, the democratic system has been adopted only technically. To say, the common citizen have been declared the highest civilian in the constitutional system, but in practice this common citizen remains very helpless, weak, poor, uneducated, inefficient and untrained in the country. In the element of any national importance such as Indian democratic system, political system, judicial system, law system, policy formation, economic development, Indian common citizens are not able to properly discharge their role. So that he could do this, the necessary strength and training for this has not been given to him so far. Bodhisattva Baba Saheb Dr. Ambedkar proposed a law to establish an accountable Parliament in India so that at least Parliament should be accountable to the people. It will be ironic that the elected representatives of the non-democratic society often forget their responsibilities and their duties and integrity towards the nation and the society.

India has been under the patronage of British colonialism for a long time. This colonialism has dipped Indian politics, Indian society and Indian psychology. Often it seems that India has been liberated from its roots and that is looking for its future only in the colonial legacy. India has been going through a 'crisis of identity' for a long time. In India, many type of societies and systems are seen moving together. The differences and the distinction between the citizens have taken a very formidable look. In India, many America, Europe and Africa are bring up together financially and mentally.

The plight of economic colonialism or the neo-colonialism cannot be eliminated unless this hypnosis is destroyed. Some developed and powerful nations have got this perception that they are authorized to make the whole world civilized, educated and cultured, and they can impose their policies as they wish on the poor and underdeveloped countries in a desired manner. It is not hidden from anyone that developed and prosperous western countries are trying to engage the rest of the world in the trap of consumerism on the basis of their falsities and misleading facts, by any means such as Money power, Military power, Media-fed publicity. India should believe in its power and strength. A nation having population worth 125 crores, that was hypnotised such a way for hundreds of years is truly a shameful global incident. Independent India will have to be free from this hypnosis. Without this, building of a capable and confident India is impossible.

Communal appeasement

Indian society and Indian politics have still not become conscious after the partition of India on the basis of religion. Even in India, narrow politics is being done on the basis of religion and caste. Even after six decades of independent India, Indian politics has not been liberated from communal appeasement. Almost all the developed nations of the world give the highest importance to national interests only. This is the reason that these nations can rapidly become so capable, prosperous and powerful. All citizens of developed nations feel themselves the same and by the state, they are treated fairly on the basis of equality. On the contrary, the politics of communal appeasement has been kept in the national interest in India, and the equality and justice cannot be established in society.

Unfortunately, in India, policy decisions and laws are executed on the narrow and self-reliant basis of 'number force' and appeasement in place of merit and national interest. This is the reason why even knowing that what is in national interest and what is not the government and the administration can't take strong decisions. Overall, this leads to the operation of anarchic and lawless system in the country, and this greatly damages national interest. At the core of the democratic system adopted by the Indian Constitution, the resolution of the operation of a judicial system was expressed on the basis of merit and truth.

Due to the politics of vote bank and communal and community appeasement, Indian politics has disinclined from the merit and the principle of truth. It is believed that there is no place of merit in Indian politics, and only communal and community appeasement can go ahead with the shortcut politics of the vote bank. This kind of narrow and broad sense of society and anti-national politics has damaged India badly.

Today, there is a very strange situation in Pakistan created after partition of India. What is the reason that Hindus and Sikhs, whose ratio was more than 20 percent during the partition of Pakistan's total population, have now become less than one percent of Hindu citizens? If the ratio of Hindus and Sikhs in Pakistan's population remained the same, which was in 1947, then today in the total population of 20 million, the population of these two would be more than four crore, but today the population of Hindus and Sikhs is less than 50 lakhs in Pakistan. The remaining three and a half million Hindus - Sikh minority citizens were forced to convert or disappeared in Pakistan. Contrary to India, minority communities are receiving full freedom and security. Even in India itself, the population of Hindu majority society is declining.

In Pakistan, where the minority's share is almost finished in the total population, after the independence of India, the population of minority Muslim community is continuously increasing rapidly. In 1951, the proportion of Hindus, in India, of the total population was 84.98 percent, while Muslims were 9.91 percent. In 1971, the population of Hindus declined to 82.72 percent, while Muslims increased to 11.21 percent. Even in the subsequent decades where there has been a continuous decrease in the Hindu population, the population of Muslims has increased steadily. Hindus are 80.5

percent according to the 2011 population, while Muslims are 13.4 percent. Muslims have become majority in Jammu and Kashmir and Lakshadweep. In these states, the Muslim population is approximately 65 percent and 96 percent respectively. In the states of Assam (30.9 per cent), West Bengal (25.2 per cent), Kerala (24.7 per cent), Uttar Pradesh (18.5 per cent), Bihar (16.5 per cent), the political parties in the states are in a decisive role.

Senior most thinker Balveer Punj, in his article, rightly asks that what is the status of minorities in Pakistan, such as Shia and Ahmadiyya etc. what is their status? What is the reason that both Shia and Sunni are safe in India than Pakistan? What is the difference in the situation that Pakistan has become free from Hindutva and in India it is still alive? Definitely Indian Hindu society is having more patience, tolerance and it is a rational society, since ancient times different types of civilizations and cultures have been cherished and flourished.

A committee of the five judges of the Supreme Court, which included Justice M H Baig and R S Sarkaria, had defined Hindutva. Quoting from Encyclopedia of Britannica, Khand Peeth said, Hindutva embraces all beliefs and worship practices rather than accepting or denying any worshiping method. The clause further said that Hindutva is a compilation of civilization and various religions, where no one is a founder or a prophet. According to the court, Hindu is used for people living in this country, even if they are not associated with any religion or community. This is our identity.

It is obvious that Hindutva is a symbol of a broad Indian lifestyle. It cannot be stacked in the narrowness of religion and sect. Indeed, Hindutva has been seen as the identity of entire India at the global level. Hindutva does not have any sense of ambivalence or competition towards any other religion or sect of the world. Due to poor politics of vote bank in independent India, deliberately misinterpretation of Hindutva has been done for the sake of mere private interests in a deciding manner. One of the strong reasons for the Hindutva in independent India is that the last three generations of the country have grown up in Nehruvian independence India. Nehruvianism was basically the name of Western uninspiration, tolerance towards religious fundamentalism and hostility toward Hindu identity. Secularism is always the basis of the social and political life of India. According to Hindutva, the meaning of secularism is Respect for all religions. It is not the standard of appeasement of the fundamentalists of the minorities.

In reality, till when there will be a Hindutva philosophy in India, until then, the values of this country's universality, integrity and pluralism would remain intact. In the part of the country where Hindutva became weak, that part was either separated from India or separatist movements took the foot. Indeed, Hindutva and democracy bilateral secularism in India are synonymous to each other.

It is a universal truth that there have been many religious and political leaders and organizations in the history of Islam in the last 1400 years, especially in the last five to six decades, who have tried to forcefully impose their fanatical and illogical thinking on others. Islamic scholar Haji Wahid, who was the three-time chairman of the highest religious institution of Indonesia, Nahaldul Ulama, rejected such tendencies. According to him, trying such a system and having such a thinking is a non-Islamic trend. Scholar, writer and columnist Hassan Nisar says that Islam requires a more scientific and logical approach. The spread of education and science can only eradicate the occupied narrowness within the society. In the absence of this, in today's world, anger, hatred, violence, fundamentalism and terrorism are being spread in the name of Islam.

It is notable that only two decades after the passage of Prophet-i-Islam, a revolt of Khawarij was born in the Muslims of Arabia. Khawarizin believed that Muslims outside their campus should be killed. It is believed that Muslims, who are conscious, believe that today's alleged jehadi-institutions are pushing the legacy of the same Khwarij mentality. Three people are the main organizers among the Khawarizin thinkers of then and now. These include Mohammad Ibn Al-Wahab (1703-1792), Syed Qutb (1906-1966) and Abul Aal Mududi (1903-1979).

Since the war against the occupation of Soviet Union in Afghanistan in the 1980s, on the heads of these three fanatical followers, the ghost of Jihad, Khilafat, Shariat, Shahadat has ascended. It needs to be understood that on the basis of violence and terror, a systematic and peaceful society can never be created in the world. Violence and terror are like a never ending blind tunnel.

By getting rid of it, a bright and radiant world can be built. According to Hussan Nissar, a senior writer and columnist of Pakistan, most of the Muslim society is still male dominated today. To maintain personal power and self-rule, the Muslim community don't believe in any ideological revolution, nor in any meaningful initiatives. These alleged personalities believe that keeping the 'terror' will help them to be remained in power, in their family system, and that should continue to move in the same way. The birthplace family of ideological revolutions, but there is no scope here. It is a streak, neither can it be small and nor can it be made larger. Only with it, can be beaten because to make it big or small is 'miserable' and its punishment is 'fatwa'.

Actually no society can move ahead by denying their history. It should be better to tell the upcoming breed that what mistakes were made by previous generations in history and what was wrong with that society and the nation that made them suffered for hundreds of years? Only then the upcoming breeds will remain alert and careful about not repeating those mistakes. Most developing countries like Indian-Pakistan are covering all those mistakes made in history. Dirt is never eliminated by putting a curtain, but only for some time it is hidden and inside it keeps on growing more fierce.

By telling the concocted stories of the superiority of the past, we are actually fooling ourselves. Due to these mischief stories of the past, there has already been a lot of damage to Indian society and nation. Now, it should not exceed. For that it is necessary to establish an educated, honest and rational scientific society. It should also be remembered that in the past, whatever went wrong or injustice happened with us as a nation and society, the culprit is no one else, only and only we are. If we have been taking advantage of our weaknesses, cowardice and mutual conflicts, if a handful of foreign invaders trampled us for thousands of years, then how can it be called 'conspiracy' of foreign powers.

If a handful of foreign invaders take advantage of our misdeeds and if they try to trample us, then we should be ashamed of this and this should not be repetitive, and we should try to eradicate those evils from the society honestly. We cannot compromise our innocence and our conspiracy of innocence and conspiracy of others. In the name of history, such lies will make us weak in the future. The developed and prosperous nations of Europe and America have come out of poverty and set out in the form of a global superpower today, because they learned a lot from history and constantly rejuvenated and trained themselves as a well-organized society.

Anti-national behavior

Recently, Shahi Imam of Jama Masjid Syed Ahmed Bukhari presented a sensational example of 'treason' by ignoring the Prime Minister of India and sending an invitation to Pakistan's Prime Minister Nawaz Sharif in the trilogy program. Of course, no citizen of India can justify this kind of conduct. In any other country of the world, if a person lives in the same country, can he think of doing this 'treason'? This kind of misbehavior and mischief is possible only in India.

  Creation of New India

By doing this, Shahi Imam has hurt not only the dignity and prestige of the Prime Minister's post, but unnecessarily also created religious communal suspicions among the citizens of the country. From Muslim organizations to ordinary citizens, each one condemned this kind of mentality. The person himself Shahi Imam's brother, Yahya Ahmed Bukhari, had scolded Imam for this act. Yahya Bukhari says that after being rejected by the country's Muslims, Imam is trying to come to the media's eye and by not inviting the Indian Prime Minister, he wants to become the Messiah of the country's Muslims. Not only this, Yahya Bukhari has even said that if Shahi Imam likes Nawaz Sharif so much, then he should have organized this jurisdiction program in Pakistan itself.

It is beyond the understanding that why this kind of mischief and national treason in India is tolerated? It seems that continuous tolerance of anti-national activities and no provision of any kind of punishment for it has become the destiny of the Indian democratic system. By the way, it is also completely wrong for Sayyed Ahmed Bukhari to make his son Nayab Shahi Imam. According to the Islamic beliefs prevailing throughout the world, the post of Imam is not virtuous, but the Shahi Imam wants to keep it for a family name. According to the rules, all the possessions of the Jama Masjid and their maintenance are under the Waqf Board, but no rules of the board are probably applicable on the Shahi Imam. If this is not Breach of trust then what is it that they consider property of Waqf board as their properties? It is a fact that the Muslims of the country do not consider the Shahi Imam as their leader.

The Shahi Imam, after all, keeps on doing this kind of anti-national conduct only to maintain the opinion of his political leader. It is also not hidden from anyone in the country that how they negotiate and support various political parties during their election. It is a fact that after the Mughal emperor Shah Jahan built the Taj Mahal in Agra, he built the Jama Masjid in Delhi. In order to oversee this mosque and perform religious activities

Shahjahan called Syed Abdul Gafoor Shah Bukhari from Bukhara, in Uzbekistan in 1656 and made him the first Imam of Jama Masjid. Since then this building of Jama Masjid was with the same family. It is a matter of great surprise that the entire world and the great empire in India ended with time and replaced by democratic systems, but it seems that the Jama Masjid of India is at the top and he is still carrying out the religious, feudal and imperialist thinking. The country ended the Mughal empire and all other empires ended one by one, even then the Jama Masjid was carrying unnecessary Mughal empire. Ironically, due to this 'distorted secularism' and the hypocrisy of the so-called secularism, most of the time of Jama Masjid is spent in doing political interventions in place of social reform efforts and religious work.

If we look at the international experience, even today, the king of Saudi Arabia employ Imam of the holy mosques, but it can also be changed in their lifetime, once someone is imam, it does not mean that he will continue to be responsible for a lifetime, or will remain in office. All Imams in Turkey are government employees. Certainly, there should not be any role of government in this process or the election of Imam in India and it cannot be done, but it is necessary to maintain democratic process or spirit in the Indian mosques present in the number of millions. It is also necessary that in this context the conscious people of the society should come forward and stop such moderate and arbitrary conduct, which is why India becomes a laughing-stock at the international level. Of course, this type of behavior cannot be accepted within the country.

Does this Islamic philosophy or ideology and its tradition allow any mosque to be used as a private property for hundreds of years? There can be no imam of any mosque in dynastic way anywhere in the whole world, but it has been happening continuously for the past six hundred years in Delhi's Jama Masjid. This contract will continue for how many years, no one has the answer to it. It should also be asked to whom Prophet Mohammad should have given the

                                        Creation of New India

authority of the mosque located in Medina to his daughter, wife Fatima and son-in-law, Hazrat Ali after his death? Perhaps no other example of this kind of chaos and arbitrary conduct anywhere else in India could be found anywhere else.

It is a bitter and bizarre truth that in India many such anti-national incidents and anti-national conduct are taken very normally, which they probably will not tolerate in any other country in the world. If such incidents occur in any other country of the world, surely they will not be tolerated at all. There are so many examples in the history of independent India which has proven that how are we careless and visually impaired of national identity, integrity and pride?

India is such a generous country, where such statements are often given, which is not in the national interest. Sometimes these behaviors are also done which no conscious and self respecting nation will ever tolerate. India's generosity also becomes a reason to encourage anti-national behavior. Since it has been tolerated for many decades in independent India, to make anti-national statements or conducted such behaviour in the country, therefore, those things are not taken seriously, which are actually very sensitive and fatal to the security and integrity of the nation.

During Jammu and Kashmir elections recently, according to Peerzada Manjur Hussain, MLA of PDP, Kashmir is a sensitive state and there would be a Hindu to make the Chief Minister against the interests of the state. It should also be asked that how can a legislator of a political party who claims to be self-righteous and engaged in public welfare, can give such discriminatory statement? If such miscreants are considered to be true, then to Manjur Hussain should be asked that how did Dr. Zakir Hussain, Fakhruddin Ali Ahmed and Dr. Kalam become the President of a vast country like India even after joining the minority community? Similarly, Dr. Manmohan Singh, who is associated with minority communities in India, how could the Prime Minister continue for ten years in India?

It is clear that India is the most tolerant and generous country in the world. The freedom and security that Minority communities have in India, it is no doubt that minorities in any other country of the world don't get it. India is a country where constant minority communities have been observed with great love and affection since independence. It is essential that politicians who try to question the issues of racial, caste and religious discrimination like Pirzada Manjur Hussain should be banned from contesting elections with immediate effect or staying in politics. Not only this, legal action should also be taken against them in case of giving such unconstitutional statement.

Education and Entrepreneurship

Most of the Muslim leaders in India never talk about basic problems of Muslims and their economic development. It has been the result of only political selfishness by distributing religious sentiments that even though the majority of Muslims in independent India are still struggling with illiteracy, poverty and unemployment. At the level of modern education and entrepreneurship, there has been no solid and effective measures for the betterment of Muslim society in independent India, and they have been persuaded and seduced by religious leaders of political parties and Muslim society themselves. It is also a matter of concern that whenever there is talk of Indian Muslims, its center is Muslims of North India. We knowingly or unknowingly do not go to the Muslims of Karnataka, Tamil Nadu and Kerala etc. and do not indulge or forget them in the discussion. The truth is that by ignoring the Muslims of South India, an overall picture of Muslim society cannot be made in India.

The Muslim community in the South is different from the Muslims of northern India in the sense that they are more educated and aware. They are entrepreneurial and have adopted the local language and culture. The Muslims of South India are doing very important and commendable work in the field of education. There

   Creation of New India

are several medical and engineering colleges of Al Amin Trust in Karnataka. There are four medical colleges in Andhra Pradesh, which are run by Muslim trust. Compared to South India, the situation of North India states is very bad. Muslim institutions are running a medical college in Delhi. In Assam, the organization called 'ERDF' is functioning, which is running many institutions and big engineering colleges. Computer education is also a feature of this institution.

Because of the education of Muslim society in South India, there are no problems in those states which are spreading in Muslim society of North India. In India, Muslim children, adolescents and youth must be made inevitably towards modern technical education. Traditional religious education given in the madarsas cannot meet the needs of the Muslim community in the modern era. In the absence of modern education, technique and technology, the Muslim youth is becoming frustrated and discouraged. They are not able to fulfill the new age of employment requirements. In the compulsion, Muslim youth has to be forced to work in small shops.

In the absence of modern education, there is lack of adequate information and understanding of modern practices in the subject of health and hygiene in Muslim society. Majority of the country's Muslim dominated settlements and the areas are seriously affected by dirt, infectious diseases and mismanagement. Many Muslim youths become toys for anti-social elements and get entangled in organized crime of serious nature. It is clear that with the help of better education, modern technique and technology and progressive thinking, at large, Muslim youth can be made co-operative with the development process of the nation.

Secularism versus fanaticism

Indian society is basically tolerant, generous and have high patience. The makers of the Indian Constitution had begun to believe that the freedom of religion and worship has to be declared as the fundamental right of every citizen of India. In the preamble of the Indian Constitution, the holy resolution has been given to all citizens to provide 'social prestige and equal opportunity'. The Indian Constitution includes the principle of non-religious discrimination. This principle is generally applicable and in the field of public employment, in particular for example, Article 15 of the Constitution has been stated- 'There will be no discrimination on the basis of state, religion, race, caste, sex, place of birth or any of these.'

Article 16 states that "All citizens will have the equal status of opportunity in matters related to appointment or employment in any post under the state." Similarly, Article 25 guarantees 'freedom of intercession and freedom of independent business and religion', but law in India does not make any provision to keep religion separate. The words 'dharmnirpeksh' and 'dharmnirpekshkaran' are the adaptations of the English word 'secular' and 'secularization'. These English words were used for the first time in the year 1648 in Europe at the end of the war that lasted for 30 years, and then they got the intellectual idea of the streamlined popularity. These are used in the context of the transfer of property to the King under the control of the King. After the Revolution of France on November 2, 1798, the Talirend (an elderly French politician) announced in the French National Assembly (France National Assembly) that all the things related to Church houses are in the possession of the nation. Several years after this announcement, in 1851, George Jacob Holeyog formally coined the term 'secularism'. The word secular is derived from the Latin word 'secular', which means the present age or generation.

The word 'secular' is related to the social process of secularization. As soon as the word 'radicalism' is mentioned, a picture of modernity and anti-liberal and non secular view emerges in our mind. Radical or new awakeningism believes its supportive religious scholar "an attempt to return to pure and original values and practices". The powers of social change have been important for the rise of 'fundamentalism'. When there are huge changes in a society and due to change in the community there is turmoil, as a result of which many people lose the values and ethics and this creates a situation of inadmissibility in society. In these situations, whatever support they get for comfort, they catch it.

The characteristic of 'radicalism' is that it always prompts the return of a better predecessor. It is difficult for people to avoid its psychological attraction. For the return of such a 'better age', 'fundamentalism' gives birth to a broad and autocratic, rigid belief system and ethics. The promise of bringing prosperity to the followers in Radicalism is inherent. Radicalism has the potential to bring a deep commitment to those who believe. That commitment is so strong that those who disbelieve are deprived of their rights. Therefore, 'fanaticism' often takes on a fierce and aggressive form where killing and spreading terror are considered both right. Radicalism is generally considered to be the opposite principle of secularism.

It is notable that after the death of Abu Bakr in 632 AD, Omar was elected as Khalifa. Osman was elected after Omar's death in 645 AD. After the death of Osman in 654 AD, Ali was chosen as Khalifa and remained Khalifa till 661 AD until he was assassinated. After the death of Ali, the Khilafat institution was over. Khalifa should be a Muslim. He should be gentle and mature. He should be a man, because only he can afford to carry heavy responsibilities on his shoulders. He should be an independent man, and not just a slave, who cannot live up to the freedom of his duties. He should be free from physical and mental defects. He must be able and brave to implement the established penalties of Islam and to protect the state of Islam and maintain peace system in the state. There can be only one Khalifa in Islamic policy. There are clear traditions of the Prophet regarding this issue. In the Islamic stories and practices allegiance to Khalifa and her government have been described as religious duty of all the citizens of the Islamic State, but this allegiance is limited and conditional, because it is only mandatory to desirableness. This is considered as the complete acceptance of Shariat's order. Unless Khalifa and Imam generally support the values of Islam and do not leave their goals and objectives, they have been told to follow the command. The principles of the Quran are strengthened by the many statements of the Prophet, in which Muslims should not obey the order of that ruler, who are against the order of Allah and His Prophet. Religious 'fundamentalists' or extremism in India is primarily a part of the medieval period.

Wherever there was Islamic rule in the Middle Ages, before the British rule, being Hindu was a crime. The Hindu had to pay a religious tax called 'Jajiya'. If he could not give it, he had to adopt Islam religion or to face death penalty. Immerse the bones (mortal remains) of your dead bodies or for other reasons tax was imposed on the pilgrimage sites of Haridwar, Gaya, Kashi, Prayag, Kumbh, Kurukshetra etc. of Hindus. Due to such long-term governance policies, there was a lot of irony in religious tolerance in India.

Even during the freedom struggle of India, Mahatma Gandhi gave a lot of emphasis on the Hindu-Muslim unity, but all of them were done on the basis of the sacrifice of Hindus. On the incitement of the British, they unnecessarily adopted the policy of Muslim appeasement without understanding, and they succumbed to the vicious move taken by the British. Due to this valueless surrender, due to the movement of Indian independence struggle and immediate political leadership, the elements like merit and truth rapidly diminished. Mahatma Gandhi's alleged preaching of non-violence was also for one-sided Hindu citizens, which meant that Hindus has to follow their Ahimsa Paramodharma in every situation. But for the Muslims he used to say that if their religious book Koran allows violence, then we can't insist them on non-violence.

Indeed, the vision of Mahatma Gandhi in the context of Hindu-Muslim unity was not proven completely. The country had to pay a heavy price for this approach. The huge India land became fragmented due to this impartiality. The demand for partition of the nation for 24 percent Muslims in undivided India was imposed on 67 percent Hindu citizens and about nine percent of other communities. As a result, lakhs of people were victims of the bloody massacre throughout India. Millions of citizens had to lose their lives and their motherland. For many decades, their generations have been deprived of basic human rights as displaced refugees, and they continue to stoop to poverty. Many victims' families have not been able to recover from this shock till today. Ironically, communal appeasement is still an inseparable part of Indian politics. It is obvious that we did not take any lesson from our horrific and destructive history. Today, the requirement is that only one religion should be recognized in national interest and it should be confirmed that religion is the 'nation religion'. In any case, any kind of nationality and anti-national work should not be protected from any corner of the country. It is ironic that in discussing any topic related to Indianism in India, it seems to be in doubt. Examples of this type of neglect to the topics of our past and national pride are not found elsewhere in the world or any other arrangement in the country.

The monarchy of this vast Indian nation has been in the hands of anti-India elements and foreign invaders for nearly 1.5 thousand years. In a planned manner, he successfully deployed India and Indian society as a nation with horribly fragmented and distorted. The possible measures for destroying the culture and civilization of India were also sustained by these foreign invaders. In this anti-national work, many anti-nationalists have cooperated with foreign invaders. These anti-nationalists invoked not only personal invitation to foreign invaders to invade India, but also assisted them in every possible way as their agent.

Even today, many Indian scholars are working for the ignorance of anti-national forces while carrying symbols of colonial slavery in the greed of wealth and false honor. In some open form, then in some pseudo form. It is essential to bring a general system to the nation. For him, it is necessary to be in the hands of the right and the nationalist citizens. Many citizens and organizations in India are engaged in the task of nation building. Their work should not only be promoted, but also for the other remaining citizens, it should also be sources of inspiration.

Blasphemy in the name of religion

If there is unrest in society in the name of religion then surely it will not be good omen for the nation. Appropriately, on conversion, there is not only a widespread debate at the national level but it also became a law, by which all kinds of conversions being done with treachery can effectively be curbed. In India, the new law should be made in such a way that in case of adopting the worship system of its choice, there is no indication of the freedom of the person concerned.

Indian Constitution gives freedom to the citizens of the country to adopt religion according to their liking. Under this right people have got the freedom to publicize their religion. On the basis of this exemption, incidents of conversion from large scale to deception are done. Hinduism, not only because of its internal weaknesses like caste system, is left behind in attracting people of other religions, but due to these weaknesses, people of other religions succeed in attracting Hindus.

Indeed, religion or creed has their "spiritual and emotional support" for those who believe in him. People's faith takes them closer to their God and this faith is stronger than religious' beliefs. In a country like India, a poor person considers religion and faith as his support, for living. In a country like India, millions of people live their lives having faith in God. This is their biggest inspiration and moral strength. If this power is taken away from a deprived, poor or devoted person through deception and seduction, it will not only be a betrayal with the person but also with the whole humanity and the nation.

To transgress citizens by greed, fear or deception must be a punishable crime. There is no objection if a person changes his discretion and voluntary worship system. It is the fundamental right of any person to express faith in what kind of opinion it is. Indian Constitution provides complete freedom to the Indian citizens on a religious basis. Although citizens of many countries of the world do not have such freedom and authority. The situation of minority communities in many countries of the world is extremely hellish and every moment they are constrained to live a life of double standards in the face of terror and horror.

The natural consequences of voluntarily leaving Islam in most of the Islamic countries of the world are different types of persecution, insecurity, economic damage and often 'death penalty'. It is clear that in these countries, citizens do not have religious freedom and they have to move on the basis of the customs of the majority community. This is the reason that citizens who have been associated with the minority community in these countries to suffer from torture and terror, have to be blamed for mass conversion. In a civilized society, can the acceptance of the conversion of others by denying others' religion, temptation or fear, be accepted in the name of the promotion of their religion?

Countries that give education to India must first self-examine themselves and take measures to protect the religious freedom of the citizens of minority communities here. India's classical conservative tradition has been a victim of fear, greed and deception for centuries. In the era of colonial rule of the British government, Christian missionaries repeatedly ridiculed the faith of Hindus for hundreds of years and termed it as inferior and low level. Christian missionaries have made extensive intervention of Indian citizens in the country. In 1941, the proportion of Hindu religious groups was 84.4 percent. The current figures should be seen in this context. At present, India's population is 125 crores.

The population of Pakistan and Bangladesh is approximately 20-20 crore people. Thus, the total population of these three countries is roughly 160 crores. Today, 80 percent of India's population is Hindu, means that there are 96 crore Hindu population. Today, in all these three countries, there are 98 crore Hindus in the world, if there are about two crore Hindu-Sikh population in Pakistan and Bangladesh. Which is only 61.25 percent of the total population of 160 crore. If the proportion of Hindus remained in line with the figures of 1941, today the total population of Hindus in these three countries should be 135 crores. This question must be asked where did the remaining 37 crore Hindus went ? It is natural that either they were killed or they were forced for unilateral transit.

In fact, conversion has been one way in the Indian subcontinent. According to Indian Sanatan culture and beliefs, every person has the right to live and choose the method of worship according to their will. In fact, the same generosity and tolerance proved to be timeless and cowardly. For hundreds of years, foreign fundamentalist movements ridiculed this generosity, tolerance of Indian civilization. The weakness and cowardice prevailing in Indian Sanatan culture have been trying to swallow the organized caste like Islam and Christianity, which have been weak and neglected by the centuries of Hindu society by taking advantage of full circumstances and beliefs. These organizations have been adopted to convert temptation, pressure and hypnosis to conversion.

It is also a fact that social reform and religious reform movement in the Indian Hindu society has been very limited. Internal hypocrisies and practices in the religion and society could not be destroyed. Vulnerabilities such as discrimination, untouchability, unrestrained and caste discrimination in Indian

Creation of New India

society have been widely used by foreign invaders. Since Swami Dayanand Saraswati's time, Hindu society has tried to imitate Islam and missionary society through 'purification' and service activities, because there is no basis in Hinduism, hence there is not much success in this area.

While Islam and Christianity are constantly trying to increase their number and base throughout the world, there is no such social or religious movement in Hinduism. Historically, Hindu society has been discriminating on the basis of caste among its own citizens. That is why the Hindu society has never been fully organized. Due to the hypocrisy of caste discrimination, service activities in Hinduism do not receive noble and desirable respect. For this reason, the popularity and propaganda of Hinduism has not been in the form of a global level, as has happened to Christianity and Islam.

Orthodoxy and terrorism

Rashtriya Swayamvak Sangh's (RSS) chief Mohan Bhagwat has rightly said that due to the collective selfishness, the struggle, exploitation, oppression, violence and fundamentalism are born. Due to such many vested interests, terrorism, fundamentalism and violence have spread widely in Middle East Asia. Due to the selfish politics of the western countries, many fundamentalist organizations like 'ISIS' have emerged in the world. Today, most of the countries of the world and a group of many sectarian groups have come into the limelight to create a collective power in protest of this crisis created by terrorism.

This aggregation is actually happening due to compulsion. To meet personal interests by global superpowers, from time to time, weapons and resources have been provided to many terrorist organizations in various minority countries. On time, these organizations naturally make themselves strong and start showing eyes to their own masters. The other prosperous countries of America and Europe today are frightened and terrorized by terrorist organizations created by them. Countries like Denmark, France, Spain, Italy, England, Ireland and Australia today are battling with terrorism. In fact, this terrorism that is changing frequently, is born from the cycle of action-reaction of the non-partial tendencies and the enjoyment of the pleasures of selfishness, without eradication of these in the whole world, the problem of terrorism and fundamentalism that has been going on for centuries in the world will not end. For this, firstly global society has to eradicate injustice and inequality everywhere. Those who want to expand their empire under the guise of peace establishment or in the name of disarmament, the nations, who try to keep other countries self-relentlessly strong, will never allow a peaceful and tolerant world to be established. Actually, it is time for every nation of the world to observe and to reflect. Of course, in this modern era of 21st century no one would have imagined that the reason for the destruction of mankind would be fundamentalism and terrorism.

Caste system in India

India's Human Classical Survey has studied 4635 communities and castes in its project 'People of India'. According to this study, there are some main characteristics of the so-called high caste in Indian society, namely- (1) Their position is highest in social order. (2) They have complete control over all resources and land properties and (3) They have non-business relationship with the following lower castes. There are also some specific characteristics of the so-called low castes, namely- (1) severe poverty, whose main reason is that they do not have land assets and have little control over resources. (2) The low social level, which is related to purity and impurity, and (3) being absorbed in traditional occupations, which are considered as unwelcome and low-level tasks.

India has many theories of the origin of the character system. Some people believe that the origins of this system were made by divine power to bring tolerance to society. According to them, a person is born in one caste. According to unscientific beliefs, determination of caste is based on the deeds of a person's previous birth. Some people believe that the character system has been born according to time, when there is an additional development of economic development. This is mainly due to economic division. According to one opinion, foreign invaders had developed this problem to subdue tribal people.

Studies conducted in different parts of the country have shown that caste and roles have been double-faced in each other. Srinivas believes that 'rural communities are divided into different classes, who have their own rights, duties and privileges. Those castes which were high and had power and privilege, those castes kept the lower castes deprived of them. Earlier, some castes feel hesitant to call themselves backward castes. Despite the fact that their economic status was weak, they feared that believing themselves backward will never improve their situation. Now this is not true, because under the new constitutional arrangements, the state has benefited these backward castes. These castes have realized that if they have to improve their level then it will be mandatory to improve their economic status. Without this, they cannot rise up in the society. For a long time in India, the following low caste people have been the basis of their elevation in society, to imitate the conduct and rituals of the so-called high caste. Gradually, due to the new constitutional provisions and the increasing use of science and technology, there is a rapid change in the untouchable thinking of the society.

While caste system in India has not ended, yet its color and presentation is changing rapidly. Now there is competition in these backward castes among themselves. For the political reasons in India, this new trend has come up in the past few decades that in various states of the country, such demands have also been demanded by certain Brahmins, Rajputs and other alleged castes that they should also be included in the backward castes, so that they can also take advantage of certain specific constitutional provisions. No social system can actually be stable and forever.

The social order changes from time to time. With the change of social, economic and political circumstances, changes in the thinking of society also occur naturally. This is also true for caste system in India.

At the level of experience, caste system has never been stable in its history. All castes are classified into categories. According to the Varna system, the place of caste in social stratification is determined by religious rituals, whose basis is an interpersonal relationship. Some scholars also believe that this system is actually related to the concept of 'pre-birth' in Hinduism, which has been widely accepted in Indian society, although this recognition has not been proven scientific or rational. In the Indian society, upper castes have kept their status elevated, yet the middle and lower castes have tried to successfully make changes in it.

In true sense, there is no form of caste structure found in entire India. Although there are thousands of castes in India, whose names-surnames are different, but there are only five or six classes in the whole country. It is important to remember that in the Indian society, clearly two different bases of social divisions are actually different from each other. There are many middle classes in India, which have no relation to production processes, but they are the source of modern Indian constitutional order, economic reform and administrative state machinery.

Caste system has become the identity of India. In Indian society, the caste system has tightened its entire social processes. Every work in India is found somewhere related to this caste system. Despite many changes and changes of time, caste system has never weakened in India. Even Christianity and Islam have not been able to escape from the caste system in India.

The Christian and Muslim communities of India also suffer from various caste-based inequalities like Hindus, although they do not find such hypocrisy and mutual discrimination. Despite the change of religion, there are already prevalent differences in them. Even after conversion, he got the same social position, which he had met before the change of religion. Through the change of religion, caste-order in Christianity and same caste marriage system, a section who has accpted is included. In this context, there are tribal exceptions in the North-East because caste has no role in their social system.

Caste discrimination is found in all the Indian Christian communities in India. This is more in the Roman Catholic community than Protestant. The main reason for this is that in the Roman Catholic community where Hindus of the so-called high castes were included in a large number, on the contrary, the peoples of the minorities in the Protestant community came in more numbers. Similar caste differences are also visible in the Sikhs. Buddhism, which denies caste system and caste based social exploitation, has not been able to keep its followers free from this exploitation. In addition to Islam religion and Christian religion the religion of the caste system, in the same way, in Sikhism also have been found. It is clear that caste has become an essential part of the religion in India.

Hinduism has traditionally been operated on the basis of character system. In Hinduism, caste groups are kept under a sort system based on the rituals of purity under four characters. Brahmin is on the highest posture in this system. After that, Kshatriyas, Vaishyas, Shudras and caste people have been kept respectively. In real life, the society is in the form of a caste. There are thousands of castes in Hinduism. There are countless subspecies within each caste again. In fact, the creation of Hindu religion has not come in the way of mutual cooperation, it has come to the point of separation. Inequality and caste classification have remained the main basis for thousands of years. Without disintegrating caste distinctions, this inequality can't be eliminated. It is certain that unless this distinction and inequality persists, the only solution of Indian society will not be possible.

Caste system

In the North Vedic period, caste has been at an important place in all social contemplations and deliberations and has a direct connection to its ruling-principle. In this period, each character was assigned specific tasks. This supreme duty of the king was to see that every person kept himself confined to those tasks which belong to his class. No one could try to reveal or disclose their own interests and could determine their personal ambition or personal goals. In the context of Indian society, it is a fact that Varanashram system upgraded society to the cost of human values.

In ancient times, Kshatriyas, Brahmins and later Vaishyas together formed kings' class. Shudras used to come in the slave class. Kshatriya- they used to show their power over authority. Vaishya was engaged in businesses like agriculture and trade, which provided economic support to the state. The priest's post was the highest. His work was to explain religion and to conduct rituals. It was a necessary condition for the state to get the political power and consume it by the priest. In symbolic form it meant that the Kshatriya political power would be obtained from Brahmin. Purohit means that the priest was the chief adviser to the king.

According to eminent sociologist G S Ghurye, there are six main features of Hindu Varna system. As-

1. The intensely partition of the society i.e., ethnic groups were such groups, which had a well-developed lifestyle. The membership of these groups was based on birth date, where there was no scope for choice or interest. The status of any person was not determined by how much wealth he possessed, but he was determined by what status his caste got in Hindu society?

Creation of New India

2. A system of planned order of social superiority or importance between the different races, ie, different castes used to work. In this framework of caste system, every caste group was given a special status.

3. The curb on drinking and social intercourse means that the very subtle rules prevailing on the kind of food the person consumes or drink, and the acceptance from which caste was prevailing.

4. Civil and religious disability and privilege of different classes i.e. Separation of different caste or caste groups in the village was the biggest sign of civil privilege and disability. Some rites could not have any race other than Brahmin. Similarly, the Shudras and other alleged lower castes were not allowed to read or gain the knowledge of holy texts.

5. The absence of freedom to choose a profession means that in general, each race considered a particular type of profession as its legitimate livelihood. The adoption of a second profession, excluding ancestral profession, even if it was beneficial, was not considered appropriate.

6. Boundation on marriage, i.e., caste groups used to marry only, but there were exceptions too. For example, in some parts of India, the person of the so-called upper caste could marry a lower caste woman. This type of marriage is called Anulom marriage.

There have been some changes in the modern system of chronological order. The most notable change in this is the breakdown of relations between caste and business. This changes occur maximum in towns than villages and more in cities than towns. Due to industrialization and modernization, many new businesses have been created, which can be called caste-free. Today, the people of the upper castes can be seen engaged in such work-practices, which were traditionally prohibited for them. For example, we can see Brahmins working in shoe factories. Likewise, the deprived communities in the East are also doing administrative and teaching work. This gap between caste and business has increased to such an extent that we can't define the caste on the basis of its relation with particular business.

Despite many social changes and economic changes in India, the caste system has maintained its influence in Indian society. Certainly the Indian society made up of many castes, sub-castes, religious and ethnic sects has been multi-layered. Hindu social order, the Dalits, which are usually part of it, are situated at the bottom of the caste system. This system has created a distinction between upper castes and lower classes, holy and impure castes. In common language, those who were once untouchables, impalpable, we call them Dalits. The Indian Constitution had called these tribes Scheduled Castes, but social workers started calling the people of these castes as Dalits. Today, in the political, social and literary fields of India, writers and scholars all use the same word .

Indian Constitution has played a very important role in the upliftment of Scheduled Castes. In the Indian constitution some of the fundamental rights have been given to the citizens. According to Article 15 (2) of Indian Constitution, discrimination of any kind with any citizen on the basis of religion, race, caste, sex, place of birth (A) Access to shops, restaurants, hotels and public entertainment venues(B) Will not be used for the use of wells, tanks, bathing ghats, roads and public rest houses. According to Article 15 (4), the state can make special provisions and arrangements for the upliftment of socially and educationally backward citizens or Scheduled Castes and Scheduled Tribes. It is clear that the Indian Constitution makers had well understood that the overall development of India would not be possible without bringing millions of citizens deprived of all types of resources in the mainstream of the nation.

○

 Creation of New India

11

Eradicate Casteism, Create a New India

If India has to make a strong presence on the global stage, then first of all it will have to make itself healthy and strong inside. It cannot be that on the global stage, that we should be established as a developed country and in this national and social life, we will be more embarrassed for India with hypocrisy, caste discrimination, superstition and segregation viruses. Despite receiving constitutional powers, it has happened many times in the country due to caste-based hypocrisy. While the country's distinctive figures, including the President, the Union Minister, the Chief Minister and the dignitaries on constitutional posts, were not allowed to enter Hindu worship places.

Due to these hypocrisy India is desperate, and even after seven decades of independence, India has become an aptitude and non-scientific choice in the form of an unqualified system. News of this effect has been broadcasted and publicized by the entire country and the media of the world. When there are such bitter experiences with specific individuals, it is not a difficult task to understand the situation of caste-based hypocrisy in remote villages in this country.

It is a matter of surprise that such intriguing incidents are not taken seriously in the country. There are no serious suggestive discussions on such incidents in society. After all, why such incidents happen, Hindu Dharmacharya, Dharmaguru and Purohit in the country do not stand vocally against caste-based hypocrisy in the society from ancient times and by creating a goal, why do not cast this demon of caste apart from society? It is certain that unless this happens, uniting the entire society in India will never be possible. It is also certain that a badly divided society and nation can never be capable, prosperous, empowered and complete. How long will this non-scientific and anti-national thinking of caste distinctions be maintained in the greed of false ego and vested interests? Therefore, till today, India and the Hindu community have not been able to achieve a respectable and strong position, which they should have acquired. In a country where so many dignitaries on such high constitutional positions can also stop rituals, hypocrisy and superstition and unable to bite his fairs. How can that nation become a world leader and how can he provide a strong and proven leadership on the global stage?

Poison of narrow casteism

Contrary to other civilizations of the world, Indian society and civilization have been deeply involved in the hypocrisy of casteism. Over time, now the different civilizations of the world have made themselves more scientific and rational, but the Indian society still rotting with this old, unscientific system with great care has cling tightly to the chest. In the way, in which people love their children, their caste is also very dear. In India good and bad, virtues and perceptions are assessed on the basis of caste. The caste based system has been done in the Indian society by the rhetoric of logicalism and sophistication. People in India worship their caste dacoits and infamous criminals on one hand and consider them as heroes, they do not hesitate even to despise the saints of other castes.

It is often said that India is a symbol of Unity in diversity, and here Ganga-Jamuni culture is a specialty of India. In this way, trying to disseminate multiplicity as a virtue has been tried in India. In

     Creation of New India

fact, it is beyond the truth. Historically, the fact has been revealed that India cannot be united as a nation on many occasions due to its diversity. Due to this separation, India has been posthumously. The international experience proves that all the developed nations in the world can be united and integrated into one government system under the same nationalism.

Finding Unity in diversity or variety is nothing more but finding mirage. India should come out of such type of hollow ideals. All citizens living in India should be mutually united with the integrated goal of empowering the nation under the flag of a single nation. Unfortunately, this determination of maturity and patriotism has not yet been created in Indian society. On the basis of personal interests, the society is divided into several stages. Both the upper castes and the Dalits are Hindus, but at the grassroots, there is a huge difference between in behavior their.

Ability based system in the Indian system has not been encouraged. Due to this, Indian system of administration continues to suffer from serious defects. Roots of large-scale corruption in Indian governance are also hidden in India's social deterioration. The wishes of the upper caste people with privilege are limitless and their own desires have died due to human rights. Therefore, the upper castes can make any kind of corruption to fulfill their boundless desires and their entire relatives, who are sitting with resources, can hide their corruption. On the other hand, the wishes of the deprived disadvantages are limited and none of their relatives are also not sitting above them to hide their small corruption.

Through the 'diversity', if the proportion of the numbers is given to all in the resources, the monopoly of upper castes will be reduced and the underprivileged will also get share in their proportion. Then the upper castes will be scared to do corruption, because they will feel that there can be any under privileged person above him, who will not hide their corruption. Disadvantages of 'diversity' will also be shared in proportion to their population and they will be able to achieve a little more. Even they will also not have courage for corruption. It is clear that by constructing a merit based, equitable administrative system, many evils like corruption can be prevented from flourishing.

A national stigma

The Central Government has initiated the Swachh Bharat Abhiyan for the next five years from October 2, 2014. The Government of India has endeavored that all the people of the country should be involved wholeheartedly and honestly in this cleanliness campaign. It is necessary for this campaign to be successful and in fact, Clean India can be created, that the centuries old inhuman and humiliating practice of scavenging in the country will be abolished immediately. This work should be completed in any situation within two years. Whatever it needs to be done for this, it must be done.

In this context, from the implementation of the existing laws in full force, necessary constitutional and other policy modifications may be considered if required. Providing every requirement related to infrastructure should be included in the government's top priority. Rather than keeping the Swachh Bharat Abhiyan limited to mere cleaning issues, it should be focused on the goal of establishing a wider 'human dignity'. Taking advantage of this opportunity, India should end the malpractice of caste and dirt like that forever.

The practice of scavenging in India is a dark black spot on the face of the country's development process. Even after more than six decades of independence, it is a matter of national shame that in the 21st century, millions of Indian families engaged in cleanliness are forced to live a socially humiliated and inhuman life. World's largest democracy, India has achieved remarkable economic growth rate during the first decade of this century and India has emerged as

                                    Creation of New India

an ideal place to work for millions of people. Along with this, India became an area of huge potential for foreign investors.

Despite all these achievements, it is not reflecting because in the Indian society, crores of people have left behind a lot due to caste based deep discrimination in all areas of life. These are the same people who were victims of caste based discrimination, and for centuries the dirty and humiliating acts like scavenging, the society put in their court. It will be said to be the culmination of humanitarian injustice that even after this, society treats them like 'the Classes which are born for carrying the filthy and sloppy work of dirt.'

The practice of scavenging is in the social evils that have come out of the centuries-old caste system. Due to stamping of the scavenger, the other people do not call them for any other work except for that work. In this way, these people have been denied the right to get honorable work opportunities. Due to the careless attitude of law officials, it has remained as a serious discrimination. Along with this, the short coming in the existing laws made to eliminate the practice of scavenging for the purpose of making it stand are the major reasons.

World's most outrageous malpractices

Scavenge is the most humiliating living scandal of inhuman, unscientific and social discrimination in any corner anywhere in this world. In India, it has been seen by adding to the issue of cleanliness rather than human dignity. The Indian Constitution ensures respect and dignity for every citizen. In addition to withstand the bite of social oppression, scavengers continue to be ashamed to face many health related problems associated with this profession.

According to the PIL filed in the Supreme Court in the case of Srinarayan, immediate death and cardiac arrest due to exposure to harmful gases such as hydrogen sulphide, methane and other things and, such as muscle and bone diseases, chronic osteoarthritis and inter-vertebral disc herniation, infections such as hepatitis, leptospirosis and helicobacter, skin problems, respiratory tract problems, and standard parameters for lung function, etc. include life-related risks.

To eliminate any doubt about the political will, the concern and commitment of the government, and the authority to enforce the law, to abolish the inhuman activity of scavenging, to eliminate any doubts about transparency and obligations, of course, a concrete action plan should be created immediately by government machinery and social institutions. It is necessary to identify the scavengers and dry toilets jointly, so that governments cannot deny the figures like this before in this serious matter.

For the liberation of the scavengers, through the technical changes, the human beings must be the first necessary condition to get rid of the direct contact of the stool-urine in a humane, respectful and safe way. Under the new law, along with the rural Panchayat and the urban, local bodies, the District Magistrates should be asked to ensure that no family should build unhealthy toilet and any outsider should not be kept for the cleaning of toilets.

In rural India where dry toilets are being used, the miserable condition of cleanliness must be fixed to end the mismanagement of handmade cleanliness. In the absence of facilities of sewer system, even in local urban bodies, workers are hired to clean septic tanks manually. Therefore, the practice of scavenging rural areas can be significantly improved only by improving sanitation methods. It should also be kept in mind that after finishing the malpractice of scavenging, the cleaning workers should be put in other works. For this, there is a need to pay attention to the proper planning of legal and policy perspective of the cleaning personnel. In doing so amending the laws for this, especially in the law for the workers employed in municipalities, governmental, semi-governmental or private companies, a clause/section 'will not be sacked from the work, but it will be a routine for any other work except for the dirty work' should be added.

Government programs for the promotion of hydroelectric toilet in place of dry toilets, free health of scavengers in livelihood rehabilitation and to provide education to their children, work should be done effectively by local bodies and NGOs. In such cases, administrative officials and elected representatives should be accountable for achieving targeted results.

The children of the free scavengers should be guaranteed free of vocational training free from government aided school education to college or job-oriented technical skills. Scavengers should be empowered to fight collectively from the centuries-old practice. People will have to demonstrate political commitment in passing new bills and the government will have to make it very soon and enact it to the implementing authorities so that they apply it immediately without any delay. Under the 12th Five-Year Plan, at the village level Panchayat and urban centers, local bodies will identify the dirt carriers on the head and release them from this work and implement the development work plan for their rehabilitation.

A monitoring committee, headed by Block Development Officer, at the block level, should monitor the village and urban centers every month. Similarly, the monitoring committee, headed by the District Magistrate on the district level, should check block work on its quarterly basis. The District Magistrate should be made accountable for it to determine the goal of removing a fixed number of people from this work. Proper rehabilitated should be done immediately for the persons to be freed from the work of scavenging. It is also necessary that the monitoring committee headed by the Chief Minister in the states should monitor the work done on a six-month basis.

Similarly, at the national level, the Monitoring Committee, headed by the Home Minister, should present the report in this context before the Parliament by making annual reviews of various states. It is clear that by adopting a targeted and timely strategy, India can be liberated from the world's most humiliating malpractice. As a nation, respect for India and the dignity of millions of citizens, such efforts should be made urgently. This fact should be taken into account in particular that the sections which are now cursed to perform abusive acts of scavenging, have not converted even after hundreds of years have suffered the persecution of Islamic and British rule.

This self-respecting class gave more freedom to its independence than its own lives. If they wanted this class, they could easily convert facilities provided by foreign governments and lead a better life. These revolutionary classes chose for themselves the hellish life, but did not give moral surrender to the foreign invaders. It was desirable that independent India should respect these heroes and patriots. There is nothing more embarrassing that in place of respect, Indian society put a scavenger basket on their heads. There is no equivalent example of such harshness, insensitivity and ungratefulness displayed by the Indian society in any other civilization and anywhere in the world. In fact it is a sin, whose atonement can probably never be done.

India; powerless against casteism

Now the time has come that India should be freed from all types of hypocrisy. It is a matter of great surprise that in the form of a nation, due to many defects which India has been forced to accept for thousands of years of slavery, those evils still exist in the society. There is no consciousness anywhere that by removing these faults, the nation should be strong and empowered. There are very few people in the country, who have the determination and foresight of empowering the nation by eliminating these bad prejudices.

It is a matter of thought that if we have to live in such situation for a day or has to face any kind of misbehaviour, then we become

 Creation of New India

very worried. We start thinking about the causes that are so sensitive because of which our dignity has been hurt. We start such efforts without delay so that we can increase our honor and dignity. On the contrary, when it comes to the degradation of honor of the nation, then such foresight and contemplation within us becomes extinct. Even after the tribal slavery of the foreign invaders for one and a half thousand years, it would not be uneasy in the country that for the reasons that this country remained the slave of a total of foreign invaders, by eliminating those defects, the eradication of homogeneity from the nation is without delay, till then nation building will be a day dream. Nationalist thinker Dr. Hedgewar said, "This entire Indian society comes into our family. Why do we feel hard to do country's work? I, my family, a very narrow idea that does not adorn this kind of person is the root cause of many problems generated in the country."

Surely today's requirement is that the entire society should be united. Every Indian, should understand the other Indian citizen as his family. On the basis of this type of brotherhood and emotional connection, it can be possible to build an organized society and a strong nation. Everybody in this country wants to know that due to the misdeeds of which this nation has been slaves for thousands of years, it is malignant– discrimination in the society, casteism and behavioral hypocrisy. This is the defect that has never allowed India to unite in the form of a nation and as a society. It is a matter of great surprise that even after experiencing so many harsh experiences and horrific consequences, why do not we feel a sense of sensitivity, foresight and determination in the form of a society and a nation? Although some people can say that there has been progress in the country in this direction and people are becoming conscious and active about the nation, but the truth is that this process is still very slow. Most of the citizens of the country are still unaware of their obligation towards national problems and social evils.

It is clear that if India has to emerge as a strong and capable nation, then it will have to utilize the huge human resources available in the country. Eligible individuals have to be engaged in the task of nation building. It is necessary that a merit based system should be created in the country, in which any Indian citizen should have an opportunity to move forward on the basis of merit and talent.

On the basis of birth only, an unqualified person continues to take advantage of the facilities, this type of misconduct should be terminated immediately. For this, necessary legal provisions should be made. It is necessary that the modern India should rise above the non-scientific caste system and adopt an unfair free system based on merit, in which every citizen of the country can contribute to the development of the country, with enthusiasm, on the basis of their capacities and abilities, as is evident in most developed nations of Europe and America, who have established themselves as a superpower and a prosperous nation by adopting a merit based system.

Became slaves due to discrimination, now full stop

Our ancient mystics and nationalist thinkers have periodically started a comprehensive and intensive social campaign to get rid of hypocrisy and prejudices in society. Gradually, the country and society has started getting the best results of these social campaigns and community efforts. It is necessary today that in every house of India there should be a national discussion every day among the family members. Every Indian citizen should have concern for the national problems.

For the nation, every citizen should have zeal, courage and desire to work for the unity of the nation. As long as this sense does not arise in every person, it will not be possible to build a strong and glorious India. There is a need to create a final war against discrimination and hypocrisy in the society. Now this war should

Creation of New India

end only, unless the Indian society is completely free from caste based hypocrisy and discrimination.

In India, many movements related to social reform have been going on since time immemorial. Such social reform movements have been continued from Mahatma Buddha to Kabir and from Swami Dayanand Saraswati to Swami Vivekananda. The vast benefits of these many reform movements may not have been possible for the country, because the nature of these movements has not been continuous and lasting in Indian society.

According to Adi Shankar, "There is only one form of God in all and the difference in man-human is only due to ignorance and impartiality. The power of this distinction has been born because of 'self-sacrifice'. If this great philosophy had been adopted in the overall social and religious way, then our nation would certainly have been guiding the world in every sphere of life. Unfortunately it could not be done.

Adi Shankaracharya visited every nook and corner of the country and while denouncing hypocrisy and superstition, he established four 'peethas' in the country. Our people know this as Sringeri, Dwarka, Puri and Badrika. After the establishment of these four 'peethas', Adishankar spent his remaining life in Kanchipuram and preached for the welfare of the living being. After sacrificing the body of Adi Shankar, those saints-mahatma continuously coming to these places and even today feel graceful, but the task of reforming society has not been done at the expected pace.

Dispersion of Hindu religion and the stigma of caste system has not yet been abolished. Adi Shankar has defined religion in broad contexts. In this sense, he did not consider religion as communal. They saw religion as divine. The achievement of religion can be done only by karmas, and they have no such belief. Unfortunately his followers have assumed the rituals as everything. The truth is that whatever needs to be done for today's transformation, in reality it is not carried by any of the 'peethas'.

At present, the person who is sitting on the 'peethas' of Shankaracharyas, the society should ask them, what are they really doing to eliminate untouchables, hypocrisy, superstitions and racism in the society? Surprisingly, the number of people wearing saffron clothing in the temples, monasteries of the country is on the rise, but the problems of society are not getting lessen. As long as the Hindu society does not end the non-scientific hypocrisy of its current caste discrimination and the problems that are arising due to caste system and sub-caste system do not solve the problem, then the Indian society will not be able to give anything to this world. Indeed, the salvation and development of Hinduism will not be from the discourses only, but it will only be possible by eradicating the purity of the conduct and the elimination of hypocrisy. Our Hindu religious leaders must remove hypocrisy and pretence in their practice.

If there is no problem with our religious leaders on the question of catering and food for the foreign tourists visiting and eating here, then why do so many dramatic and ritualistic behaviours at the end of our worshippers after coming home? This leads to the feeling of unbelief among the common Hindu citizens towards religion. After all, in India, why does the need to wash the place where our monks sit first at Ganges? Why do our Dharmacharya likes to visit his house only after seeing the financial, social, political and administrative status of a devotee?

Today, Christianity and Islam are probably moving forward in the world, because caste-based hypocrisy and discrimination are not rampant in the offensive way. Continuous service in Christian religion and especially in downtrodden areas, missionary and charity works are given special importance and encouragement. With these actions, this religion has succeeded in generating the charm of the citizens of other communities. Why not our Hindu Dharmacharyas are trying such a thing? Today, the issue of conversion everywhere in the country remains a matter of grave discussion. For the chieftains of Hindu religion it should be a matter of thought that after all conversion from Hindu religion to other religions has been happening and is still happening.

These has been always talks about foreign invaders and the fearful conversions arising out of it. On the basis of temptation and service activities by Christian missionaries, the topic of conversions has been rising, but the truth should also be acknowledged that Hinduism has not been able to treat hypocrisy, caste discrimination and other prejudices throughout time. This is the reason that most of the Hindus are not satisfied, happy and proud with their religion. Whose responsibility is it to change this situation? Should this work be left to the foreign powers only? Why not the Hindu monastery and the Dharmacharya make the final battle for the eradication of this hypocrisy. It is also noteworthy that often these Dharmacharyas themselves do not behave like this that they can keep a sense of common Hindu faith towards them.

There is also a charge against Hindu religion that here religion has been made a 'business' and 'trade'. In place of the spiritual upliftment of a person, religion is remained a shop, where a person is being taken as a sub-devotee and is being fooled by it in every possible way. Is religion merely a tool to pick the pocket of our devotees? How will the sense of unity in society and the country be created due to the shallow behavior of this type of economic greed? It is a matter of thought that only in this country, God has incarnated from time to time and most of the time, most of the thinkers, intellectuals, sadhus and ascetics have been born in this country, Nevertheless, this country has no good to this day. Even today, this nation is the nation with the most deprived, hungry, uneducated, dirty, discontent and inferiority complex of the world. Of course, the alleged contractors of religion in India should rise above the role of pick-pocketing and seriously do self-analysis about the social and national interests.

In fact, it is the only major cause of casteism and hypocrisy due to which India has not been able to acquire the specific place and honor at the global level so far, which could be a natural entitlement. This question should be asked why don't the Dharmacharya and Shankaracharya of Hinduism embrace a Dalit? Why can't we eat with them? Can't we create a qualitative and misleading society by providing caste-based security? How long will the unqualified marks hit on high posts for personal economic and social benefits? It should also be asked that when Hinduism will be established as a qualifying religion, in which a person will receive respect and responsibility on the basis of merit, not on the basis of merely birth?

○

12
Endless Saga of Non-Equality

After many social, economic and political changes in independent India, many sociologists had started saying that now the castes have survived in India only politically and their social existence has ended. On the contrary, the incidents and crimes that occur in society show that the elimination of castes from Indian society is still only a daymare. Our mind is still socially the same, where the primitive society lived. In the order of civilization and development, the journey of spirit's development still seems to have gone away somewhere. Suffering humanity and the incidents of racial atrocities that persecute the mind persist in the society. Such incidents make question marks on the existence of civilized society.

Many experiences of Indian history are lying with shameful examples of caste differences. Even after hundreds of years with such examples, Indian society is not ready to take any lesson. Many times it seems that we are still standing there, where many thousands of years ago we stood. In the past several decades, a lot has been changed in the country and the world, but this disease of Indian society has remained so far.

When Chhatrapati Shivaji captured a large part of Maharashtra, no priest of Maharashtra was ready to do his coronation. In the end, Gangabhatta of Kashi got ready after a big 'dakshina', but he did with the thumb of right toe instead of right hand thumb. Because Shivaji was not considered Kshatriya from anywhere related to the chapters of the Varna system. This incident of 1674 AD is recorded in historical texts with its entire humiliation.

Even with the Chhatrapati Sahu ji Maharaj, the descendant of Shivaji, the society behaved like this. When Sahuji Maharaj used to go to bath in Vanganga in the morning, he used to read the mantras of the Puranas in place of his holiest Vedic mantras, because he was non-Kshatriya. One day when Sahuji Maharaj came to know this secret, he reserved the post of priest for Prajapati society and sent him Kashi to study Sanskrit. Since then, Kolhapur's Priest was of this society. In order to bring the marginalized society to the mainstream, they were motivated by this incident and implemented reservation in their states.

When Baba Saheb Ambedkar drank the water of the lake under Maha Satyagraha, then that pond was purified. Disturbed by such a disgraceful conduct, India's Constitution's creator Dr. Ambedkar had said, "What is this society, which allows dogs and cats to drink water in the pond, but it gets polluted if it is drank by human." This sad story of absurdity forced the scholars like Ambedkar to change his religion. Once Babu Jagjivan Ram unveiled the statue of Dr. Sarvanand in Varanasi, it was also purified with Gangajal.

Even today, the post of a priest in society is reserved for the caste. Shankaracharya's post is also reserved. Although devadasis were kept for exploitation in the temples, they were supposed to be from the down trodden section of society. Swami Dayanand Saraswati had raised questions about idol worship due to these many reasons, then he was poisoned under conspiracy. The top post in the country's oldest party is still reserved for the Nehru family. All these reservations and privileges, which promote non-equality, question the maturity of our democracy.

It is the need of the hour that India should come out of those old stereotypes and unscientific thinking, due to which not only have we been humiliated by foreign invaders for thousands of

 Creation of New India

years, but even today, in the international world, other nations still do not honor us due to these dogmas. Due to this stigma of caste system, India has become very disgraced today and is still being humiliated. What is the compulsion that the Indian society is not ready to improve even after its worst condition.

Final war against discrimination

Reservation Policy is a tool for the upliftment of Dalits in education, employment, political representation, entrepreneurship etc. Although this policy has not been implemented effectively in the field of education and employment. The Dalits who got the benefit of reservation in education and employment are in a better position and they have emerged as a new middle class. Despite all constitutional remedies, racial atrocities are an integral part of the life of Dalits. Since the Dalits have started fighting for their rights, they are facing a lot of humiliation, and are being tortured.

The reality of Indian society is that caste is dominated by every aspect of life and Dalits of the Varna system are the biggest victims. It has been proved that due to caste system, a qualitative social and administrative system has never been determined in India and due to its adverse consequences, India has had to endure the long-term hardships of thousands of years, but till now the Indian society has not been able to free itself from this stigma.

It is unfortunate that there has been a handful of people in creating casteist mentality in India, on whom the Constitution and the system had the responsibility to end it. Often, the governments and the administrative system in India seem to have a very careless attitude in terms of this serious malpractrice. Recently, the Rajasthan Government has given an undisclosed amount to the intermediary marriage party to the government, and reduced the fixed tenure of two years to one year. It is worth mentioning that Rajasthan is in those states, where the majority of the people have accepted their behavior that recognized the untouchables.

In many other states of North India, there is a similar situation like in Rajasthan. In these states, the need for establishing the values of eradicating racism and equality is on the top priority. Today, there are such antisocial and anti-national preacher in the land on which the great men such as Gautam Buddha and Kabir were born for eradication of inequality and hypocrisy; those who openly say that nation and society can never get rid of caste system. Many times in India, some self-appointed experts are also found to be counting the benefits of non-scientific caste system. There have been many obstacles in the path of Indian development in the form of a nation and society, but the barrier which seems to be the most difficult and impenetrable is probably the casteism.

Until there is caste system, the country will lag behind

It is a matter of contemplation that when such serious and devastating problems exist in Indian society and nation, so why our religious gurus and religious institutions do not come forward with full resolution in the task of nation reform and nation building. Why can't our religious places revive the nation? Why can't our religion site collaborate in the structure of a welfare society? Today the fraudulent, hypocritical rituals are there in most religious places throughout India, after all, why can't these be removed? Ritualism is not extermination, but if rituals are not in accordance with practicality and they cannot adapt themselves to the conditions of the country and circumstances, so such rituals are ultimately proven to conservatism, superstitious and unscientific traditions. If rituals bind us with chains of customs, hollow them, then such rituals must be utterly abandoned. These rituals and hypocrisy have thrown the renaissance of Indian society and nation.

From the religious places, the stream of humanity, nationalism and best thought should flow everywhere in the society, but this is not happening in India. Most of our religious places are being imprisoned by such wealthy ritualistic persons, there is nothing to

Creation of New India

do with the actual values of religion, and that is why this place has become a defective consciousness, unscientific, and miserable transmission center. Most of the Godhead seems to forget the best practices and life values.

Now it is time that all the religious institutions and religions of the country should be brought under the purview of the law while investigating the wealth assets raised in the name of religion and superstitions. Today, this institution has become the medium of black money. Today, the religion of most of the ashrams, madrassas, mosques or dharams in the country, there is nothing to do with ethics and spirituality, yet their penetration in the society is increasing constantly. Under pressure of law, many Baba, like Rampal, Asaram, the siege of the rioters and their supporters has already happened, but in the future people are not caught in the clutches of such criminals, for this society should also come to differentiate between faith and superstitions. Such hypocrites need to challenge the country's constitution in the future, for this, the society and the country's politicians need to self-assess during the situation.

Most saints and great men in India have recognized renunciation and manliness as the basis of their life. His life has been an example of renunciation and mortification. Even in the world, they remained away from the trap of temptation and materialism. Now there is an army of such religious leaders who are running a business in the name of religion, doing luxuriously and displaying egoism. These most alleged religious leaders and religious godmen have made palatial fortresses in the name of ashrams and religious institutions. Not only this, these Dharmacharyas have collected the weapons. There is a long line of such religious teachers, who do not have anything to do far away from their saintly deeds.

Incest and fornication have become an integral part of their daily lives. Some of these have also been screwed up on the law and they are arrested in numerous crimes and are in prisons. Today, many vicious people of criminal propensity are pretending to be religious leaders becoming dominant in the society, making money or making fun of them. Actually, it is only an effort to become a part of the power structure in the society. There has been a flood of religious leaders at most of the country's religious shrines, who had to leave home and village due to their criminal activities. There have been many murders so far in the egoistic power struggle of Mahantai and Mathadhashi at different religious places of the country. The situation is that even now, not only in politics, but also in religious areas, nepotism has become dominant. Mahants of different monasteries want to leave their will to their family only. Finding the meaning of the monastery means wealth, social power and authority over a multitude of devotees.

It is a matter of surprise that why the top saints like Shankaracharya have been silent on the aggregation of these criminals on the behalf of the sadhus in the country? The voice against such criminal elements should arise from the saint's society, otherwise the distinction between right and wrong will end. The common man's dilemma about religion will get worse. People in our country have always been wandering about to quench spiritual thirst. Only a few of them succeed in getting the correct path, while most of them fall in the hands of hypocrites.

The saint society must find a way that people are not trapped in the clutches of such polities. It should be asked why and for whom are the Palatial and font like Ashram being built? Why the illegal occupations of land are being done in the name of the ashrams? Why is it messed up with the faith of innocent people and why is there an open mingling with the Indian constitution, and law and order? From a variety of new cases coming out, in India the prestige of saint society has been threatened.

Often, the conduct of the so-called saints who have been taught to relieve their devotion and temptation, does not match their own statements. They themselves preach in the atmosphere of luxury

                    Creation of New India

in the giant pandals. Their programs are heavily promoted through newspapers and media. As soon as the morning goes on television and on many channels at the night various kinds of Baba jumps in. Whole day keep their insights of being superior to oneself in a new style in their own way. Many such religious teachers, saints and babas like Nirmal Baba have come in 'market', who are presenting the new 'product' to the public. Almost all Babas have different interpretations about God and in order to prove their interpretation, they constantly try their new approach every day. In India, today the field of religion and spirituality has become the most popular stress-free industry.

Various charitable institutions have been created by these alleged saints to show their image better in society. All marketing modes are being adopted to increase the number of devotees. For polishing their image and Image Branding, they use to consult even the salaried experts. Overall, this kind of conduct has increased the distrust of the so-called saints in Indian society. Even at the international level, it is making the image of India as negative, conservative and unscientific country. The biggest loss of society due to these hypocrisy is that the right and qualified spiritual person has also started feeling humiliated and frustrated and the society and nation are not getting their real benefit.

The nationalist Maithilisaran Gupta's famous line, in which he says - 'He is the real person who dies for human beings.' This is the only feature of Indian culture. This culture develops the holy spirit of 'Bahujan Hitiaay and Bahujan Sukhaay' and 'Vasudhaiva Kutumbakam'. There should be no difference between 'Self' and 'on' within us. Getting out of the narrow boundaries of 'Self' and sacrificing itself for 'on' is the true humanity. This is the greatest quality and it is the biggest religion of man.

All the great men, in India, have taken care of their character from childhood itself. The goal of all the big philosophers, thinkers, sages, writers and leaders, has been to spread the human qualities by creating nation-building, but when seen in their lives, it is clear that they were all great and specific in terms of character. They never allowed their character to become contaminated. In Indian culture, there has been a singularity of totality. An explicit affirmation to give priority to community interest in place of personal interests lies in Indian culture and its discussions.

O

13

With the Same Spirit, Veneration of the Nation

In the name of freedom of expression, a new culture of continuous roles and demonstrations is evolving in India. Most of the demonstrations are political. Still, in our country, the demonstrations & mass gathering is not upto that level if related to the common people problems. Recently in India, youth struggled on the roads to safeguard the subjects such as freedom of romance and kissing as their basic rights. It would have been better if this youth of India used his power and abilities in creative movements to develop nation.

After all, why social and cultural movements never exist in our country, for the misuse of public properties and the irresponsible attitude of the citizens, dirt, open defecation, illiteracy, mismanagement in religious places, misdeeds of abbesses, fetus killing, no creativity in art and music, environmental pollution, intoxication? Why these stimuli does not arise in India's energetic youth? The young generation of India has to think that what is their duties for the nation and the society? This reflectivity, awareness and activism will prove to be far-reaching not only for the nation, but also for their future. When there can be a mass mobilization of many types of unrestrained and anti-national and anti-national subjects in the country, so why can't the society unite and create a movement on the issue of nation building?

Nationalism

'Rashtradharm' is in fact the feeling of citizens in any nation, under which citizens consider the nation as paramount in comparison to any other idea. In a way, this can be called the option of 'nationalism'. The meaning of 'nationalism' is by providing citizens 'highest importance' in comparison to any other vote. The way to move forward for any country depends on the level of 'nationalism' generated in its citizens.

For thousands of years, the nation's heroes who have upgraded nationalism have been on the national horizon. By this inspiration, India has kept its pride in the form of an unbroken celibacy. Indeed, Indian 'nationalism' is also ancient than Rigveda. Indeed, this was the 'nationalism' that was the motivator for freedom struggle. During the freedom struggle of India, millions of Indians gave Nationalism more than their lives. Thousands of revolutionaries happily sacrificed for the nation while singing Vande Mataram. When the foundation of Independent India was laid on the sacrifice of lakhs of nationalist martyrs, it was hoped that as an independent nation, India would give a legacy to its heritage of 'nationalism'.

It was hoped that the whole world would be bowing to the magnificent personality of India and the glory of freedom, but unfortunately it could not happen. The feeling of 'nationalism' has become very weak in an independent India. The eradication of 'nationalism' first started from the political sphere, but after that the rapid erosion in the nationalist values also measured the social and psychological boundaries of India. In fact, the sacrifices made by millions of revolutionaries of the country for the sake of independence its value was not even given by independent India.

In the first decade of Indian political independence, instead of 'nationalism', it was shifted to 'casteism' and 'nepotism'. Unnecessary politics of non-essential issues began to be started instead of the interest of the nation. The country was briefly entangled in the dangerous battle of forward class, backward class and minorityism for mere political vested interests. Nationalism disappeared in the storm of personal interest. Thinking about the nation and the symbol of nationalist ideas were systematically put on the margins. The appeasement politics made national symbols untouchable. Public interest issues are inexpensive, selfish politics has pushed a lot back to work. The fundamental factors of economics, development, poverty and national prosperity continued to flow out of the political agenda very fast.

It is very surprising that in the country where millions of devotees have sacrificed their self-interest and all their lives for the sake of independence, in the same India, after the independence, from where these 'bacteria' and 'virus' came that within a decade of freedom the Indian politics and social life were completely misguided. This proves that although we attained independence, but we couldn't understand our pride, responsibility and real goal as a nation. Did we really qualified for 'self-governance'? What even today, we have not been so matured and responsible that we can govern the country's rule better. This situation has persisted for several decades. Many nations like Israel and China in the world who became independent after us or almost became free with us, today, we have gone far beyond all spheres of life. India as a nation and 120 crores citizens living here should have enough thought and atonement for this. It will not be easy to replenish it. The time India had to build its infrastructure and its mental and charitable creation of its citizens, that precious time, we have lost.

Even today, many social evils and hypocrisy are spread across the country. To get freedom from them, the whole country needs to stand united and stand against them. There is a need to eradicate all types of inherent selfless and characteristic weaknesses from Indian social and political life. Whenever discrimination is done on the narrow grounds of caste, religion, region and language in the country, it promotes disqualification and chaos. This weakens the morale of qualified and talented people. It is clear that no nation can move forward by breaking the morale of its hardworking, meritorious and capable citizens.

Whenever the loss of religion and nation is expected, then the war becomes inevitable. Although every effort should be made to combat the war, but it has a limit. Treatment cannot be done by keeping the self-esteem of the nation on hold. Indian nationals should always be ready for all types of sacrifices for the revival of nation and society. It has also been clarified in the Mahabharata's 'Industry Festival' that all efforts of peace before the war will be done. Hindus, Muslims, Sikhs, Christians or any other religious person cannot separate themselves from the national boundaries while being a citizen of this country. It should be noted that any work, which is anti-national, cannot be 'Dharmsammat'.

Why being slave of 'profit' and 'greed' ?

Today, most of the problems have been generated in front of the country only because the average Indians have become slave of 'economic benefits' and 'greed'. It requires serious contemplation and churning on how and when such weakness in character has entered the country? Why have we become so addicted to extreme security on this land of sacrifice and oblation? Today we are living a life like this, as if we have won Kaal and we have become immortal for eternity. Considering the objects as the main, our entire life and attention has been confined to the collection of them. Apart from this, there is no other goal of life.

How can things and different types of consumer products finally become an alternative to high values of contemplation, philosophy and national consciousness? Can a person's life and his goal be limited to merely raising and living? Not at all. Most Indian citizens are today victims of indiscipline. Due to indiscipline, we are not able to achieve the desired success in every field. The country has to suffer the consequences of nonviolence and indiscipline. Why can't we be happy in national interest? Looking at the problems of the country, why, as a citizen, should we not sincerely discharge our responsibilities?

It is necessary that the citizens of the country start raising themselves Brahma Muhurat in the morning and in tune with Indian consciousness and philosophy. It will have large, broad and far-reaching advantages. With this we will be able to make better use and utilization of the precious time of the morning. If every person gets one hour of health in the morning, one-hour for cleaning of the house and give an hour to 'collective labor' in society and national interest, so that the whole country can be clean, healthy for self and prosperous. For this, in reality, 'self-consciousness' and 'self-motivation' are needed. If India has to be clean and healthy, and prosperous and capable, then only government campaigns and government machinery cannot produce desired results. Citizen consciousness is capable of delivering holistic and sustainable results to the nation.

Today, the basic thinking of democracy has gone astray. In the narrow sense, today the country's democratic system has been restricted to fighting elections and somehow winning the election. In most political parties, embarrassingly, family politics is a formidable form of politics. In the time of sycophancy and factionalism, the qualified citizens and the people having national consciousness are being disdained. Pedestrianism has reached its peak due to vested interests. Good statements has been reserved for Television debates only and there is no place for the 'ideals' anywhere in private practice and personal conduct.

Indian politics is battling today with fierce contradictions in 'Saying' and 'Doing'. It is natural that all 125 crore citizens in the country cannot be completely elected at any one point. It can be understood at the level of human behavior, but there is no question of not having a single opinion on the assumption that the nation is the 'head'. Nation should be paramount for all citizens of the country. There is as such no agreement of any kind is possible in this context.

Nationalism is the supreme religion

The 'nationalism' is actually higher than all the prevailing and existing religions. We cannot weaken the nation only for economic benefits. For this, we have to be very serious at our every conduct. Indeed, 'nation building' will not happen in a few days, months or even a few years, but it is a constant, eternal and continuous process. Just as a healthy body and muscles will not be created just by eating nutritious meals or going to gym, one needs to adopt disciplined lifestyle for many years continuously. Have to do yoga continuously and take a healthy life while eating healthy food, and if this sequence breaks down, then all attributes and achievements will end soon. In fact, 'nation building' has to be permanently placed in our daily life, routine, contemplation, karma, thoughts and conduct. It should be continuously and with staunch feeling retained permanently. In this way, we have become disturbed by self-pride and victory.

In Indian culture and meditation, the notion of human and God being united is expressed. For this human being must be united, without this the nation cannot be threaded in one formula. Citizens bound in the meager boundaries of ignorance, unscrupulousness, impartiality and vested interests should now become essentially united by discharging nationalism. In history, we have sacrificed many times 'national interest' for personal ego and selfishness. It is the time has come that personal arrogance and self-interest should be sacrificed for 'national interest'.

As a nation, we need to display more awareness, a solidarity and confidence. Today, a strong and prosperous country like Europe and America has been able to become powerful because they have set a skilled governance system based on 'merit', 'equality' and 'nationalism' by getting rid of superstitions. If India has to take inspiration from the West, then it should take a resolution to create such a social system based on merit, equality and nationalism.

Creation of New India

There is a need to create a human and scientific system based on skill in each area of the country. It will be better for national interest if it's complete as soon as possible.

Emancipation from amorphous

After independence many such efforts have been missed in India, which are very essential for any independent nation. It is very necessary for a nation to be liberated from the cuffs to increase the confidence of its millions of citizens. In the Indian citizens, the sense of responsibility and dignity towards the nation can be developed permanently; such efforts have not been done seriously immediately after the independence. Even after being a new independent nation, the country's man was abandoned in a chaotic and vaporized manner. The new generation born after independence was not given education of nationalist values.

Indeed, India's first Prime Minister Jawaharlal Nehru did not have specific information about Indian culture and philosophy, and he was unaware of the elements that could give the nation the feeling of glory. His ignorance made India 'non-indigenous'. Even after him, the governments that have been ruling in the country have endorsed this feeling of dullness and lack of self-confidence as a nation, that looks at foreign powers in taking decisions and is not capable of taking firm decisions in 'national interest'. Without making the country out of this sick and ill attitude, it will not be possible to build a strong, capable and powerful India.

It may be possible only in India in the whole world that the national flag, national anthem, Vande Mataram and national symbols are being insulted in different parts of the country. Why such a situation arose and why the harsh actions against such anti-national elements could not be taken? This is a matter of serious thought and concern. Islamic State in certain provinces of the country like Kashmir, Hyderabad and West Bengal.

And hoisting the flags of Pakistan and organizing the Games on various occasions, the slogan of Pakistan Zindabad is a serious kind of national treason which can never be tolerated. It is necessary that the anti-national elements should be taught a harsh lesson.

It cannot be that a person consumes food and water of India, living in India, earning livelihood and enjoying complete freedom, but his consciousness and psyche are anti-national and its activities are secretly or openly nurturing anti-national agendas. The patriots will not tolerate this kind of campaign and why should they. The political leadership of the country and territories should work firmly in accordance with this national sentiment and the administration should be given the freedom and encouragement to take strict action against anti-national elements.

On the psyche and behavior of any country, its historical and cultural heritage has a profound effect. Countries like India, who have been slaves of foreign powers for thousands of years, have a deep impact on this legacy. This long term period of slavery has seriously disrupted our language, thought, behavior, self-esteem, politics and administration and creativity. It has also ruined our memory. We have also forgotten that we were at the peak in almost every field of civilization and culture and were distributing this world philosophy and science to this world.

In fact, today the main goal of India as a nation should be to regain its lost consciousness and cultural heritage. The result of long-term slavery is that there is a rivalry in the Indian middle class and upper middle class to make itself a Western culture. The educated upper class of India does not see itself connecting with Indian consciousness and thinking, its full thinking, education, books, interests and contacts have been completely absorbed in foreign language and foreign thinking. In this sense, it is a matter of contemplation whether we have actually attained freedom in ideological and cultural form?

   Creation of New India

Identity crisis

Freedom doesn't mean mere political freedom. It is much wider than this. Actually freedom is not only related to its flag, parliament, constitution, but it should also regain perception of lost 'cultural consciousness' and 'national pride'. However, the inferiority of being treated by others and being culturally superior to the things imposed by others, can never give us the joy of real freedom and self-identification. After achieving political independence, our goal should have been for cultural and intellectual independence, but even after six decades of attaining independence, no effort has been made in this direction. After independence, the Manas children of the British captured the power of the country in the absence of inferiority and ignorance, and they presented themselves as ideal for the uneducated and poor people of the country. In fact, it was misconception and dishonesty, which, as a nation, kept us mentally handicapped and impoverished from the very beginning. On that historic night of August 15, 1947, as the country's first Prime Minister, Jawaharlal Nehru, when the country's 300 million poor and illiterate people first addressed in the English language, the common people of the country living in self-centered and sentimentality could not even understand that the country what really changed when you were free? Neither language nor thought, neither thought nor method. Yes, it has changed so much that in the place of the British, the power of the country came in the hands of Indian-born people, although they were as foreign and western in thought as much as their predecessors, the Englishman. It is a stigma in the history of the country that the British rule that we can uproot from the country after the sacrifice of millions of Indians, after the removal of that colonial rule from the country, the Prime Minister of India was using the same long-term slavery in his first address. More than this, the subject of shame could not have been anything else for the free India. This address has already filled the whole taste of newly acquired independence for nation's crores of devotees.

Before that, when Dr. Rajendra Prasad became the President of the Constituent Assembly in 1946, one speaker after another addressed him in the English language. In fact, this was 'ideological victory' of the college. Before 1947, Nehru had strongly criticized the colonial administration system or bureaucracy, Nehru did not only remain fanatical after independence, but made him more powerful. Even today, many heritage of British colonial heritage has been working in the same form in the country. In the Bengal Club of Calcutta where Macaulay lived during his stay, the permission for admission of Indians was received in 1959. The British continued to be the president till 1966 in this club. Even after independence, in many clubs established by the British for many years in the country, the notice used to hang out of the gate, the 'Dogs and Indians are Not Allowed' was written.

For many decades after 1947, the statue of George fifth has been set up under the umbrella of India Gate of Delhi. After removing it, we did not put any other image at that place, as if in our view, none of the best intellectuals or intellectual talents better than George fifth. By doing so we have demonstrated our intellectual bondage and mental bankruptcy. Even today, 80% of roads, buildings, and public places in the important areas of Delhi are being named after the British. This proves that we have not yet broken the mental chains of British colonialism.

Even today, the same ego quote in the country, the policies of the policymakers, the same running ambassador cars, the work of the highest and higher judiciary, the same English language on the files, and away from the public, the same egoistic feeling of being self-centered is universal. The same kind of giant bungalows, who make fun of the country's 80 million poorest citizens, are instantly telling the endless story of the intellectual slavery of our governments. This type of devastation has killed our cultural consciousness as a nation. For years after Independence, the elected

Creation of New India

governments of this country have been vulnerable and constantly watching this slaughter of national-cultural consciousness.

Disgrace of Indian symbols

After independence, in the country and the said high-ranking upper class has given many writers, literary, journalists, administrators and politicians to the country, who openly spent the entire life of English and Western culture drumming down and condemning Indians. It is another matter that after this, they were considered as 'hypocrites' and western countries never respected such an 'anti-nationalists' nor did they accept them.

Even after six decades of independent India, neither Hindi language nor the country has attained the status of the country nor there is a shortage of such people in the country even today, those who do not feel themselves connected to this nation's flag and national anthem of this country. Even today, Macaulay's Manas sons feel a great difficulty in speaking Vande Mataram and Bharat Mata ki jai. Indeed, this great achievement of colonial rule will be said that they have snatched us from our language, our contemplation, our lives and our pride towards the nation. The great heritage that we should be proud of, instead we are experiencing shame on that.

In fact, if Macaulay was alive today, he would certainly be surprised at the level of this mental slavery of Indians, that has deeply penetrated in them. Surprisingly, because, he would never have imagined that his English education would not only remain so far in India even after many decades, but it will continue to increase to the extent that the average Indian will start hating their mother tongue, their lifestyle and cultural heritage.

India should understand that the education system that Macaulay gave to India was a major part of the plan to maintain the ideological and administrative edge of the colonial rule and the continuation of power. Indians have also forgotten that Indian education and Indian educational institutions were the only center of knowledge and research throughout the world for more than 2000 years ago from the education system of English education and Macaulay. Today we have forgotten that the world famous Nalanda University was established in 427 AD and this university was the largest and best university in the world at that time. In Nalanda University, hundreds of teachers and more than 10,000 students were constantly engaged in study and teaching work.

At the time when education and reading of philosophy, language, research, inflammation, science, etc. was happening in India, at that time most of the areas of the world were not available for elementary education. In time, Nalanda University was destroyed in 1197 by the foreign invader Bakhtiyar Khilji and completely destroyed. There were so many books and textual material in this university and it took much time burning of this material. By forgetting its great historical heritage, today it has become a 'duplicate' by losing its originality in the field of Indian music, art, research, science, technology, sports, writing, cinema and theater. It is also a matter of thought that why is there a lack of ignorance and a sense of pride towards them on a wide level towards the actual national heroes and national important dates and events? In the name of political power, naming of innumerable public places and institutions of this country etc. have been done in the name of individual. After the name of Indira and Rajiv Gandhi, the outer and inner circle of Delhi's Connaught Place, Khuswant Singh put one was satirical in his column, "It would have been better if the name of Connaught Place was given as Maa-Beta Chowk. Due to the constant influence of power in independent India, the importance of Gandhi and the Nehru family has been found as much comparison to the other real national devotees, revolutionaries and freedom fighters.

After Nehru, Indira Gandhi remained the Prime Minister for a long time. After her Rajiv Gandhi and Sonia Gandhi's indirect

   Creation of New India

authority on central political power has been proved. During non-Congress governments for three years during the Janata Party rule, Morarji Desai fought continuously with the intervention of the government and the party. In the meanwhile, during the prime ministership of Vishwanath Pratap Singh, Chandrashekhar, Deve Gowda and Gujral, the Central Government could simply run only with no achievements.

In the third term of Atal Bihari Vajpayee, the discussion of re-writing the history of India started for the first time in the country. In this way, for the first time in the country, apart from Gandhi, and Nehru family our country started looking forward towards other nationalists and inspired. For the first time, the effort to bring their nation-building works and continuous struggle in front of countrymen was started. Although it was not possible to adjust the comprehensive, institutional, ideological and psychological imbalance in 50 years in a short span of five years. It is also a fact that the Vajpayee Government relied on allies. In independent India, another bad trend is appearing in the corridors of political power. The bad practice is the misuse of official properties and buildings at large scale and their misnomer. After all, how long will the government bungalows and institutions get converted into monuments and research institutes in the name of political persons, under political pressure?

Today many government bungalows in the country are occupied by various types of institutions, NGOs, etc. forcefully and in a wrong manner. If only one monument can be sufficient for the remembrance of thousands of soldiers who were martyred, then why should there be a separate monument in the name of politicians in the country? In this context, a clear national policy is needed in the country.

Due to political reasons, in the feudal manner, the misuse of national wealth of the country cannot be allowed to go on for longer periods of time. After all, why memories of Nehru, Indira,

Lal Bahadur Shastri, Jagjivan Ram, Kanshiram, Charan Singh etc. cannot be saved in any monument? Bungalows have also been allocated in the memories of Rajiv Gandhi and Sanjay Gandhi along with Nehru and Indira. Why can't the Rajiv Gandhi Foundation and Sanjay Gandhi Memorial Trust be operated by Trimurti Bhawan or Indira Gandhi Memorial? In the name of dead political persons, this government loot which has been steadfastly running for several decades has to be stopped mandatory.

According to senior author and columnist Rajeev Sachaan, "If the memories of the big leaders are going to be saved in the same way in the government bungalows, then the day will come when the Lutyens zone of Delhi, would be inhabited by the dead souls." To save the memory of the family members of the senior political leaders of the country, the 'Lutyen Zone' in Delhi is often the most 'appropriate' area. It is worth mentioning that this area is probably the world's most expensive area. In the twenty-first century, the level of knowledge of the country's masses has become so much that he could understand what research is being done in these monuments and research institutes based on the names of dead political persons and what are the benefits to the country from those alleged memories and values? It would have been better that the monuments of dead political persons would be built by their relatives and followers with their personal wealth and contribution.

○

14
Atonimation of Historical Mistakes

In India, it is now being expected that perhaps due to planned efforts in the country, the contribution and struggle of many real nationalist, revolutionaries and freedom fighters will be given due respect and representation. Properly, the central government has started the task of making the public aware about Sardar Patel's actions, thoughts and struggles. The Gujarat government has made provision for the budget for the 182 meter high statue of Sardar Patel on the river Narmada. On his birthday, the message of unity in the country has been given through organizing programs like 'Run for Unity', on all India basis.

For many decades, during the long reign of Congress in India, all the leaders outside of Nehru-Gandhi family were pushed to the margins. Sardar Vallabhbhai Patel and Dr. Bhim Rao Ambedkar were awarded Bharat Ratna several decades later. Literature and writings of Nationalist thinkers like Patel, Ambedkar, Swami Vivekananda, Madan Mohan Malaviya, Dr. Rajendra Prasad, Dr. Shyama Prasad Mukherjee, Deendayal Upadhyay and Dr. Hedgewar were also not encouraged in independent India. The views of these thinkers were not even allowed to reach the Indian public. The national views, because of which, as a nation, India, and the Indian people could have gained huge benefits, were denied then.

From Dr. Shyama Prasad Mukherjee to Deen Dayal Upadhyay and Nanaji Deshmukh, who worked firmly on the concept of nationalism other than the ideology of the Congress, the government deliberately did not pay any attention to it. President of the Indian Constituent Assembly and the first President of the Republic of India, Dr. Rajendra Prasad, was also not given proper place and honor in the independent India. The people of the country were deprived of their ideas and literature. Similarly, many nationalist revolutionaries and freedom fighters could not get that honor, importance and respect in independent India which was expected.

The present Government of India has started taking lessons from many of these mistakes in Indian history and has been prompted to correct them. Several National schemes have been started in the name of Shyama Prasad Mukherjee and Deendayal Upadhyay. The Government of India should strive to take a fresh discussion on the various issues that have remained neglected so far, which have been neglected by the Indian History and Research Council and research institutes.

The local historic national heroes who strengthened national consciousness in North and Southern states, need to provide special importance and place in educational courses and various government and other policy plans. By doing so, 125 million Indians can be encouraged and motivated towards their responsibility towards nation-building works. In his Vijayadashmi address, Sir Sangchalak Mohan Bhagwat remembered the great ruler of the country, Rajendra Chola. Rajendra Chola and Hemu fought many wars against foreign invaders and defeated them.

In the 21st century educational courses of independent India, the real National heroes, freedom fighters and martyrs, namely - The work of Sardar Bhagat Singh, Lala Lajpat Rai, Bal Gangadhar Tilak, Ashfaq Ullah Khan, Maharshi Arvindo, Swami Vivekananda, Sardar Patel, Dr. Ambedkar and Dr. Ram Manohar Lohia etc. should be brought to the Indian public. After the independence of India, the process of denying truth due to the effect of the contaminated politics of the vote bank in India started.

Due to its side effects, after achieving independence, nationalism was denied in India. The Indian political leadership, who had been exposed to the illusory colonial-eradenic English-language ideology, and after independence, also experienced Indian political leadership with mental slavery disorders, for many decades, real nationalist discussions in India and the country's fundamental intellectual property was not allowed to flourish. After achieving independence, the Indian political leadership should at least have to follow Mahatma Gandhi's ideas.

Gandhiji on 6th October, 1946, wrote an article on Harijan and warned that, "If we can produce our own land instead of donation of foreigners, then the ability and courage to live our life on it, capacity and courage should be developed in the nation's citizens, otherwise we will not be entitled to live like an independent country. "In reality this idea also applies in the context of imported colonial, English-Western thought streams. Due to these imported ideas, Indian political leadership and power establishment have become mentally ill. The wide impact of these thoughts has also been felt on Indian opinion. Imported ideas should be accepted to the extent that they can be useful and beneficial for us. National thinkers and national personalities are not the property of any political party or organization. A single right cannot be accepted on any particular issue. Indian nationalist thinkers and national heroes are equally revered for the whole nation.

Era of national renaissance

"Hum Kaun The, Kya Ho Gaye Aur Kya Honge Abhi?
Aao Milkar Vichaar Karein, Milkar Ye Samasyayen Sabhi."

Means, Who were we, what has we become and what will happen to us now?

Come let us think together, Together all these problems...

These lines of Maithilisaran Gupta are still relevant today, for the national life. The idea of Akhand Bharat was done in that era, but over time, the feelings of regionalism and separatism have been developing in the country. For the creation of a capable and powerful India, it is necessary for the citizens of this country to be free from such narrow feelings. There is a need to make special efforts in this direction to create a better environment in the country. Many 'mantras' of the era of freedom struggle have become again relevant today. Imperialism and colonialism are being fascinated by the new colors and shapes. Many elements that are contaminating Indian culture and values are becoming effective today. Due to the increasing consumer hypothesis of consumerism and western culture, the roots of Indianness are becoming weak. In the explosive era of economic liberalization, some major countries of the world are deciding on all the rules and regulations for other countries of the world. In fact, the face of imperialism keeps changing constantly at the practical level. International experience also proves that it does not end with the end of the direct colonial or military rule, but this expansionist 'trend' of governance in different forms remains in the society. In the modern world, the spread of this kind of tendency can be easily assessed. Even today, there is an expanding tendency of economic, cultural and psychological imperialism in most of the world.

In fact, the era of globalization for these imperial forces and has been proven to be more beneficial. The first colonial rule used to make other nations slaves on military power cable and then they used to plunder and torture them badly. In this economic age of the new globalization, there is no need of military power. With this, the cost of the competent and developed nations is being saved. Now they are plundering many countries without spending any money. The cleverly developed Western nations have worn this trend of their robbery with legal cover. The universal process of liberalization is actually reinforcing this trend of pillage of colonial nations. The result of this psychological imperialism is that in

1997, the Prime Minister of a country with a large population of 100 million was bowed down without giving any thought in front of the British Empress in the Common Wealth Conference.

The meaning of 'Nation' has been very broad in Indian charm. In the context of Indian thought, 'microstic' is considered a factor of 'collective'. Just as the main unit of the building is a Brick, in the same way, the basic unit of society or country is person. In the society, where the majority of people are exposed to the rituals and conduct, the same will be the nature and behavior of that country. On the contrary, if the mindset and ethos of the vast majority of people are going to lead the anti-national and society downward, then that nation and society will certainly fall. When Mahatma Gandhi had said after independence, "The President of the country should live in shabby area, this is my wish". In his core, it was the feeling that the first citizen of the country, when leads a life of simplicity, frugality, virtue and sacrifice, of course, this positive impact will definitely be on the rest of the society.

India was fond of making 'Tain Tyakten Bhujitha:' that means sacrificing from an ancient time. Not only this, by saying 'Ma Ghrudha: Kasyaswidhanam', the saints said the wealth does not belong to any person or any family, wealth is of nature, this great idea was established before the society. It is the eternal truth that no matter how much wealth, power a person has, when the journey of life ends, his entire wealth and power remain on this earth.

Indian philosophy has been "Idam Na Mum Idam Rashtriya". In fact, everything belong to the society and the country, this feeling should be within us. In our country, those who put the philosophy of 'simple living, high thinking' in their behavior, them consumerism and the ongoing storm of profit and greed must certainly be the point of contemplation for us. The Products has made an edge over ideas in our social life today. In fact, during the colonial rule after a long period of several hundred years, the British had separated India from its original rituals with a very careful planning. The plan of the British' crooked policy to make Indian citizens valueless, rootless and traditionless has been very successful.

Construction of able India

The level of consciousness towards the nation is evidence of being disciplined for a citizen and with a liability towards the nation. In Indian social life it is often seen that we keep commenting on the behavior of the citizens, the behavior of the prevailing ideals and social beliefs. Certainly Indian society is a very conscious and active society.

After achieving independence, in the last six decades, in the way of continuous political, administrative and social change in the Indian mindset has strengthened democratic values, proves the wisdom of the Indian public. At the level of individual, region and community, Indian citizens have been showing their activism and sensitivity on most occasions. Every day, many examples of such type of activity and sensitivity are found in the country.

Although this activity of most citizens in the works of broad social interests and nation building does not appear with the expected enthusiasm. In Indian society, people who are neglected about family and community are often publicly condemned, but in the context of this consciousness, condemnation and sensitivity of the nation and the people who neglect the society, the occupancy vanishes. There is a need to make continuous efforts for the creation of discipline-bound society. Unless the citizen who is standing at the last step of our democratic system is distressed and suffering, till then, it cannot be claimed that the nation and society have been in the overall development.

Of course, today it is necessary that every citizen should give the highest importance to the nation and abandon all types of private self-sufficiency in provoking national security. It is also necessary that every person should understand that his other liability also comes after his discharge of responsibility towards the nation. It is obvious that if India is not as dignified, safe and uninterrupted as a nation, then no citizen of it will be able to protect its personal interests.

Though a positive and constructive environment is slowly and slowly being created in the country, but the common citizens of India also need to understand that the picture of the country will really change when it will come forward to discharge its obligations in national interest itself. In order to awaken national consciousness among the citizens, the Prime Minister is talking about repeated public participation. He is repeatedly telling people that in the case of education, health, cleanliness etc. he should introduce his responsibility and make a constructive endeavor to empower the nation as a vigilant nation.

Today's awareness and activism about its rights and facilities is being seen in the general public, if the same awareness and activism arises in most citizens for national interests, then India can be established in just a few years as a fully developed global superpower.

With the governments in nation building, citizens also have a very important responsibility. Many vulnerabilities and nationalist organizations have been working in the country from time to time to awaken the task of this civic responsibility. In addition to monitoring the governmental activities, citizens should also see how they can make a creative contribution to the activities and events of nation building? Comprehensive public participation is mandatory to solve many social problems available in the country.

It is clear that when the talks are of India, creating India, for India's interest, then there is no need to discuss about other interests. Any kind of personal, economic, political and community interest cannot be more than India. Today the requirement is that by eliminating all kinds of differences, every citizen of the country should have one and only one goal– to build a 'Capable India'.

Historically and traditionally, in India, positions and economic solicitation have never been given much importance in the society. In Indian society, only those have been acknowledged as a vandalistic and ideal, who completely abandoned personal pleasures and interests for the wider interests of the nation, society and humanity. Such great figures have always been considered exemplary in the country. In India, many spiritual figures and social workers have always been receiving greater importance, respect and support from powerful politicians. Even today, in the social and political sphere of India, the people who are able to fight for creating a clean image for society and the nation are getting more support and significance.

Mahatma Gandhi also understood the importance of civil society. Despite receiving all the power and support, he did not accept to sit on top political post after attaining independence. Certainly his trust was more on manpower and wider social national values. Likewise, Lok Nayak Jai Prakash Narayan also kept himself separated from the political posts even after being the basic foundation of change and leadership.

There have been many such occasions and instances in the history of the country, when many Indian dignitaries gave high honor and priority to the work for the nation and society instead of posts and power even after having full strength and support. It is notable that Dada Dharmadhikari had refused to become the Chief Minister and Union Minister. Similarly Krishnadas Jaju rejected the proposal to become the Finance Minister at the Center. At that time he was the president of the Indian Charkha Union. He declined saying, "There will be many qualified people in the country to work for the finance minister, but there is probably no one who can work for Charkha." Similarly, Gandhian economist J.C. Kumarappa refused to become a Member of Parliament or a Minister, because in his eyes social workers have a decisive role to form a strong nation.

　　　　　　　　　　　　　　　Creation of New India

It is clear that from the beginning only Bharat Bhumi has been the work place of many Karmyogis from Buddha and Chanakya to Kabir, Chaitanya, Dayanand Saraswati, Vivekananda, Mahatma Gandhi. Many such examples have been filled in the history of the country, when the nation's Karmayogi, the devotees, have given the nation highest priority instead of personal interests and power.

Disciplined India

The proper use of the resources of the country, its savings, all these liabilities are in fact belong to us, and in this direction, we all have to maintain a healthy and active effort. Some rules of discipline must be established in personal life. Without doing so, proper utilization of national resources and essential savings of national natural resources will not be possible. For example, due to the need and availability of huge population in the country, crisis of energy and oil continues to be clearly visible.

They should be exploited only in proportion to the natural resources available in India. Now, it cannot be that the thing which is lacking, is being spent on luxuriously indiscriminately and continuous availability forever and ever in its country. This kind of behavior cannot be called foresightedness.

In fact, for the proper utilization of natural resources, every Indian must discharge its 'civic religion'. The luxurious abuse of those items which are continuously lacking in the essential natural resources of the nation is destructive for the future, but clearly it can be given the name of a 'treason'. For the saving of petroleum products, oil and energy, the average Indian will have to work in his personal life. How to conserve these natural resources more and more, such behaviors and observancy should be adopted by Indian nationals in daily life. With a little bit of physical exertion and contemplation of the nation, India can make its future safer.

Fearless India

For the creation of a nation, every citizen must fully suppress all kinds of fear, greed, inferiority complex and cowardice within himself. Swami Vivekananda had said, "All distrress is born from fear. The horror person is similar to the deceased. Fear is the source of all kinds of evils. On the contrary, the fearless character has the power to find a way out of great adversity. Fear is a specific type of mental slavery. Just as the slave continues to suffer for the sake of independence, the same fear of the person is also restless.

Fearless behavior is a necessary condition for nation building. Due to cowardice and fearlessness, India was not actually developed for thousands of years as a nation, and it remained tight in slavery vessels. The same nation is able to prove its power in the world, whose citizens discharge their responsibilities by being brave, courageous and fearless, to face the challenges.

The fearful person becomes free of all types of creative creation, self-confidence and skill. On the contrary, the fearless citizens continue to make the nation proud by earning all the mentioned achievements. It is clear that fear of the future denies us from the present. Often we are afraid of telling the truth and cooperating with the truth that this can make some people angry and may be harmed to us.

Keeping the ideals and values at stake, any effort of self-respect reduces us in our own eyes. It should be understood that life is fleeting. Nobody has come to be immortal on this earth. The person's conduct and ideals can be maintained continuously relevant to society and nation. The courage to speak the truth and walk with the truth is actually our basic identity as a human being. If our morale is high and will power is strong, then it can definitely be easily liberated from the personal selfishness and fear caused by it. In fact, we need to be afraid of those actions which harm the nation and our soul is dull.

 Creation of New India

As a nation, India has experienced the continuous slavery of foreign invaders for the longest period in the world. It should be known that due to the cowardly conduct of the people of fear, India, despite all its capabilities, has been in tandem with thousands of years. Indian citizens were frightened by the sword of the foreign invaders, and this fear destroyed their intellectuals. Due to personal selfishness and due to its fear, they became so distraught and misguided that they did not even remember that they were in crores and if they had courage, so these cuffs of slavery can be thrown in a moment and thrown off.

In fact, those foreign invaders should have been in fear, who, despite being ruthless, kept trampling the land for thousands of years and kept seizing it uninterruptedly. This proves that fear and cowardice are not only deadly for the person, but fear also put civil society and nation down. Today, the nation which has become the head of the world, they were not even in the map of the world some hundred years ago or were struggling with slavery, but with the bravery of citizens, today, this nation has become a great power of the world with courage and unbroken karma yoga. Indian citizens need to consider why they cannot raise a little bit of courage, to free themselves from the enslavement of thousands of years and stand here today, where many other powerful, prosperous and developed nations of the world have stood.

Worship of the Lord Nation

Certainly this time is the worship of the nation only. Nation Dharma should be the only and supreme religion for Indian citizens today. Similarly, Nation God should be the highest venerable and revered God or adorable for every Indian citizen. Swami Vivekananda's call was for "Nation's worship" and "If only for the 50 years, our motherland, India will become our adorable, then India can be established as a great nation." He used to say that until this goal is achieved, till then there is nothing wrong in the removal of our Gods and Goddesses from our brain. Put all your attention on this God. Our country is only our awakened God. His hands, legs and ears are everywhere. Think that the other Gods and Goddesses are sleeping. Those worthless God and Goddesses we can't see them, we are constantly running after them, and we are not doing the adoration and veneration of the great Nation God which we can clearly see everywhere. When we worship this evident God, then only we will be left to worship the other Gods and Goddesses.

If we study the global system, it becomes clear that nationalism has always been receiving the highest importance in comparison to all the other religions. Most of the nations in this world are seen to be inclined to the spirit of nationalism. How strong is this feeling of nationalism, it can only be estimated from the fact that the three broad world-wide views, such as Islam, Christianity and Communism, which are determined to bring down the entire world under a single flag, by invalidating the boundaries of countries, has not been able to eradicate the spirit of nationalism from the world. On the contrary, these ideologies have embraced the form of different nationalities and adopted the same color and form.

Today, the form of Islam in Turkey, Egypt, Iran and Indonesia is not the same. Even though there is same religion in every country, but their form is different from each other. To maintain their distinct identity each country has accepted different sects of Islam. While Iran accepted the Shiya cult and adopted a different Islam from the Arabs, at the same time connecting the beliefs of ancient Parsi religion with Islam, it gave Islam a new look in the form of Sufi cult. If Turkey gave a special form to Islam by sitting in harmony with Western civilization, then Indonesia assimilating the effects of Indian culture and shaped its Islam in a different form.

The British gave birth to the Protestant form of Christianity by rejecting the power of the pope of Rome, who took the resolution of establishing the Divine Empire in the whole world. Similarly,

 Creation of New India

Luthran and Syrian cultures were established in Germany and Syria respectively. Dutch, French, Russian etc. citizens also accepted Christianity in different forms in their own country. The nature of communism, who dreamed of establishing the dictatorship of the proletariat all over the world, has also been different in different countries of the world. In Russia, China, Vietnam, Albania etc. communism is of very different nature and is also confront with each other. Clearly, this experience of various nations proves that in reality the feeling of nationalism in the whole world exists in the citizens in the most powerful form. Every citizen has a flutter and the highest sensitivity towards his nation.

Every citizen of the world, of course, wants to see his nation as strong and special. It is clear from this that nationalism has the capacity to raise the entire citizens of the country in a single form by rising above the discrimination of all kinds of religions and races. For the country with problems like India, there is only one way to salvation- strong nationalism. If more than one billion citizens of the country could be made up of national consciousness, then within a decade we could establish India as a global superpower.

India is not a personal property

It is unfortunate that after attaining independence in the country, India was politically held hostage to a family. Internal democracy remained dead for several decades in a system that claimed to be a vast democratic country and society. This is the period when there is continuous erosion of democratic values in the political and constitutional system of the country. The solicitation, vandalism and loyalty of a family specialty became the standard of merit and the national interest and constitutional goals went somewhere in the direction. Due to this contaminated trend and conduct of continuous nurturing in independent India, six decades of freedom is achieved and despite having full potential and capabilities, India has not been recognized as a self-sufficient and developed nation.

Today it is the demand of the time that India, like the nations America, China and Germany, make nation the center of highest importance in each of its political modes. In place of national interest, when personal interests are given more importance by the political and administrative system, then it is impossible to achieve the goal of overall national development.

Unnecessarily, in the independent India, more than 450 programs and schemes of the central and state governments have been named after Rajiv, Indira and Nehru. This is a distorted form of 'political feudalism', which may not be found anywhere else in the world. The names of the major 20 schemes introduced by the previous central government have been named after a family special.

Namely- Rajiv Gandhi Aawas Yojana (for cities), Rajiv Gandhi National Rural Electrification Scheme, Rajiv Gandhi National Drinking Water Scheme, Rajiv Gandhi National Scheme (for the benefit of working women), Rajiv Gandhi Udyami Mitra Yojana, Rajiv Gandhi Shramik Kalyan Yojana, Rajiv Gandhi Shilpi Health Insurance Scheme, Rajiv Gandhi Panchayats Empowerment Abhiyan, Rajiv Gandhi Equity Savings Scheme, Rajiv Gandhi Rural LPG Distribution Scheme, Rajiv Gandhi Kishore Yuvati Empowerment Scheme, Indira Vikas Patra, Indira Canal Project, Indira Gandhi National Old Age Pension Scheme, Indira Awas Yojana (for rural areas), Jawaharlal Nehru Urban Development Plan, Jawahar Lal Nehru Employment Scheme etc.

22 of the 26 names of various events, competitions and awards related to sports were named after Rajiv Gandhi, while the remaining four were named after the name of Indira-Nehru. 10 international stadiums are in the name of Rajiv Gandhi in the country, while six are in the name of Indira and one is named after Jawahar Lal Nehru. Similarly, nine of the country's airports or seaside are on the name of the Nehru family. There is no count of such educational institutions, whose names have been named after the Gandhi-Nehru family.

In the name of Rajiv Gandhi, Indira Gandhi and Nehru, there are more than 200 universities, colleges, inter-colleges, colleges of technology and other educational institutions. List of awards, scholarships, grants for research work, parks, sanctuaries, hospitals, medical institutes, name of the buildings, name of roads, name of streets, name of villages, etc. is so long that a complete book can be written.

Karmayogi Bharat

Karma yoga is actually the best yoga. Work is worship. There are few such human gems in every country, who do karma in true sense. They do not care about name, neither achievement nor fame. They work only in national interest because of which the country will move forward. Most of the citizens in the developed countries understand their responsibility and are engaged in national work. These citizens are happily doing their work with responsibility and all the small tasks in the national interest, i.e. cleaning the house, the roads and public places. In fact, the nation is not created merely by the activities of some of the great devotees and great souls, but it is done by the cadre of the lakhs of crores of citizens and the general cognition, which inspires them to do every small task in the national interest.

If India is free today, that is because of the contribution of millions of unnamed nation devotees behind this, who did what was to be done with this limited resources for the national interest. Some people are also those who, with a higher aim, move forward to help the poor and the human race, because they believe in the welfare of the nation and the society. Even today, lakhs of patriotic citizens in the country have been sacrificing their lives in the work of nation building only. It is clear that whenever a citizen will work with selflessness for the nation interest, then much more superb results will come out.

Virtues such as renunciation, patriotism, love, truth, and selflessness are not mere figurative descriptions of morality.

In reality, this quality is the ideal of our social life. Not doing aspiration while doing karma, and even after helping a person, it does not have any kind of gratitude to have great human qualities. Similarly, by not doing any good deeds, do not give any notice to whether he will give us success and karma, this is the toughest but exemplary fact in this world. Regardless of the condemnation of people around you, it is always the biggest sacrifice in the work of nation building.

The real character of a great man can be found only by karma and conduct. Contingent opportunities also give small and young people some kind of nobility, but in reality, the great one is the one whose character is always superior, valued and equal in all types of situations. The power of karma is the most powerful and decisive in man's life and this Karma yoga has a lasting influence on man's character and conduct.

$$\bigcirc$$

15
Side Effects of Mental Slavery

A sad fact in the context of India is that in the form of a nation, India has continued to ignored its pride and historic dates associated with national leaders. It is a side effect of thousands of years of long-term slavery and mental slavery of colonial rule. There are many dates and opportunities which can enhance the confidence of Indian nationals and the pride of the nation. India should celebrate the dates of national importance like December 16, with full dignity and festive spirit throughout the country. We often forget the dates associated with national pride. This trend can't be said auspicious for a dignified nation. In fact, it reflects our lethargy and dull thinking as a nation.

The day of December 16, 1971 in the modern history of India certainly has special significance. In the context of Bangladesh war, this date symbolizes Indian bravery. Recalling the bravery of Indian soldiers, it is remembered as Victory Day. In that war 3,843 Indian soldiers were martyred, while the number of wounded people was three times more than this. 1,313 soldiers who participated in that war were awarded posthumously Gallantry medal. Four of them were also honored with Paramveer Chakra for showing indomitable courage at the war land.

Unfortunately for the last four decades, these great heroes of 1971 have been deprived of their natural and justifiable credentials of their victorious and justified victory. Field Marshal Sam Manekshaw, who led the country in this war, died in 2008, the then government did not give that level of dignity and importance to his funeral that a nation's devotee should be given. The work of making war memorials of our martyrs has not been taken seriously in India. Probably in any other country of the world, such a worst condition of our heroic soldiers and sacrificial nationalists would hardly have happened. Of course, this situation should be changed.

The whole nation must bow towards heroes and their sacrifices. Whatever can be done in this context, it must be done. Now, there should not be any further delay in this. From the point of view of national pride in India, many examples of dumbness and lack of farsightedness have been observed. India has been unnecessarily respecting the war heroes of the enemy nation in an extremely irresponsible manner. Can a normal person even imagine that the book of an Indian hero of Kargil or a war with Pakistan before it, in 1965 or 1971, should be released in Pakistan? But this astonishing behavior was done by India.

Many times it appears that we become moderate to the extent of Indian stupidity. We allowed the book of Pakistani warrior, Flight Lieutenant Arshad Sami Khan of 1965 war, to be released in Delhi. Similarly, Parvez Musharraf, who is guilty of an audacious Kargil war, has been invited not only in various seminars organized in India, but also on his engagement with Delhi, the Indian media has been proving to be boastful. This type of inferiority complex, lacking farsightedness and dumbness need to be overthrown by its behavior. The nation and its citizens will not realize self-esteem themselves, they can never become eligible for honor on the global stage.

Adornment of nation hero

Though worshiping God and praising His glory is done everywhere in India, but lag behind to honor many such Karma Yogis, who actually work for the country. It is an indisputable truth that India has created such a large number of thinkers, intellectuals,

Creation of New India

philosophers, scholars, solitaire and spiritual men, that has not given by any other country in the world.

It is amazing that many times we forget about the teachings and their contributions. In fact, national heroes do not have any class or caste. They win and die for the nation. It is essential that the entire nation should assess their contribution on this basis.

It has also been noticed in the country that there has been always a dispute in the elections of eligible persons for most national honors and ornaments. In fact, these national honors and ornaments should be kept free of personal political interests and other pseudo-agenda of any kind. The nation's deceased nationalists should be eligible for real honor on the land of India. Going ahead in this direction, the Government of India has taken a commendable step by deciding to confer Bharat Ratna to such nation's devotees.

To honor Madan Mohan Malviya, a great national thinker, the Government of India has taken a wise decision, though delayed. The introduction of the vision of 'Mahamana' Pandit Madan Mohan Malviya can be narrated in this example that when the whole country was in dilemma even after fighting for freedom, Mahamana had the perception of independence and thus founded Banaras Hindu University (BHU) in 1916. The requirement of engineers and technical experts for the development and reconstruction of an independent India, the country's first engineering college was established in the university in 1918.

Mahamana was such a great monk, who established a huge educational institution like Banaras Hindu University for the future generations only by seeking donations from people. The specialty of Banaras Hindu University campus, spread over an area of 1300 acres, is that there is a system available from primary to higher education in the same campus. To make Banaras Hindu University a prosperous center of education, Madan Mohan Malaviya persuaded the then superior teachers to Banaras Hindu University.

In this, Dr. Sarvepalli Radhakrishnan, former Vice Chancellor of Banaras Hindu University was also involved.

Madan Mohan Malaviya's personality was a reflection of Indianness. As an advocate, he saved 150 convicts who had been sentenced to hang in the historic Chauri-Chaura case against the British rule in Gorakhpur. Leading politicians of the struggling Congress for freedom struggle, patriots, social reformers, teachers, educationists, editors, river Ganga and Cow devotees, Shrimad Bhagwat and Geeta's unique scholars, Karmayogi, speaker, lawyer etc. they have dedicated their whole life for the development of the nation.

Against the ban of the Ganges stream coming out of Gangotri, he started a comprehensive Satyagraha campaign under Ganga Mahasabha. Eventually, the British government was compelled to compromise and it was decided not to build any dam or factory on the river Ganga in Uttarakhand. Authentic facts are not available in this regard, who gave Malviya the title of 'Mahamana'. Probably Mahatma Gandhi called him 'Mahamana– A Man of the Large Heart' during the 1916 Calcutta Congress convention. Malaviya, who was an important soldier of the independence movement, had also attacked the British's 'divide and rule' policy by establishing Hindu Mahasabha at the same time.

Madan Mohan Malviya stayed with the Congress for five decades and became its president four times. He also laid emphasis on improving caste system and poor state of women in Hinduism. He considered journalism very important for national and social change. He played a key role in implementing Hindi in the working of the courts. Madan Mohan Malaviya put forward the excellent way of achieving the journey of development and modernism, along with religion. He also well understood that not only spiritual but also a strong educational system can be the basis of any country for cultural, economic and industrial development. Despite all these priceless national contributions, it took so many years to give India's top civilian honor. This fact is surprising, but in the list of Bharat Ratna, there have been many such names, who were remembered for a long time. Years later, the selection of 'Mahamana' cannot be called too surprising.

The selection of best individuals in a country with vast and cultural diversity like India is not so easy. Probably a special class of person having the power of money, public and publicity, he himself should start declaring a specific person to be entitled to Bharat Ratna, but this does not mean that the entire public of the country also sees him in this form. Indeed, the protagonists of the publicity are somewhat different, whereas the ideal heroes who create a place in the heart of the national mind are different.

There have been many such great and ideal personalities in the country, who made significant contributions in different areas of life. Despite this, they have not received any respected ornaments till date. Despite not getting respect, these great personalities worked a lot. Crores of people are their followers and admirers and they keep on moving their ideas. The best way to honor folk heroes among the public is to extended their work. The values of their lives should be spread and their ideals be moulded by the citizens of the country in their conduct.

○

16
Creation of a New India

"Kaliha Shayano Bhavati Sanjihaanastu dvaapara!
Uttishthanstreta bhavati kritum sapaghate charan!
Charaiveti! charaiveti!"

It means, the person who is asleep is a 'kali'. The sleeper who is awake from sleep is 'dvaapar', but the one who start walking, becomes an 'era', 'Satyuga' and 'Swarn Yuga'. So it means– Keep on walking, on walking. It is clear that the conduct of the citizens of a nation is the basic determinant element of the superiority of the ages. Karmayogi citizens can only bring India to 'Satyuga' and 'Swarna Yuga' with their conduct and courage.

In fact, nothing is more important than the nation. No person, neither any group nor any state etc. Those citizens and institutions who are deeply involved in luxuries and selfishness can not save any nation. In fact, neither they have any attention on this side nor are they capable enough for this. Why is it that there is a continuous crisis of pride in the nation? Our borders are still unsafe and in many areas India has not been able to achieve the expected achievements yet.

Even smaller countries are moving forward in the race of development in compassion to India, but the awareness, restlessness and anxiety expected from the Indian citizens, the governments, the society and the administrative system has not started appearing. Considering the current state of the nation, awareness of citizens is essential. It is unfortunate that the citizen of India is still not conscious, alert and not fully competent. Our discomfort and anxiety towards the nation is still not adequately visible. The unity of the nation is very important because adversity and difficulties never comes by giving advance notice.

It should also be realized that the security, prosperity and development of the nation is not a celebration that every citizen will be invited for it. Protecting national interests is the primary responsibility of every citizen living in India, whose feeling should be observation, repetitive. As a nation, we should know that a nation is more important than traditions. This nation must necessarily be redeemed by the unscientific stereotypes, traditions and inertia that reduce the power of the country and increase the inequality and distinction between the citizens.

The nation needs capable citizens. When the question is the security of the nation, its prosperity and its interest, then turning its back on the citizens for its responsibilities will be called Treason. Keep in mind that if the pride of the nation has eroded, then nothing will remain. The identity and glory of each person is related to the nation only.

As a nation, in this country, on the issue of 'national interest', many harsh experiences with the patriotics have been continuously being seen in past years, on which no sensitive and patriotic citizen of this country feel proud of India. In the last few decades, as a nation and superior life values and traditions, India has been broken and shattered. This image of India, as a nation and society is that it has been unable to protect its traditions, culture and values. Why is it that India has been continuously tolerating anti-national activities and anti-nationalists for the past several decades? the big question is: When India was, as a nation, how and when, under what circumstances did it become so helpless, constrained and weak?

Today, the ignorance, the escaping away from responsibility and the deterrence towards the nation are increasing. The characteristic weakness of the impatient citizens, busy in earning only, and embarrassed political system where politicians are hungry of political status, is being reflected everywhere. It is often seen in India that there are conflict over many small things. In most of the citizens, there is so much more sensitivity about personal dignity that ordinary and often trivial things also become 'a question of prestige'. Similarly, Indian citizens are very sensitive and aware of the interests and respect of caste and community. The 'question of prestige' started on the smallest issue, soon after a few minutes, takes the form of community conflicts and riots. This conflict, which started on the point of insignificance, increased the scope of the area within a few hours and then flooded the whole city and several cities in riots. It is clear that Indian citizens understand the question of prestige and the sense of pride. Even the Indian citizens are more sensitive and alert to the question of reputation and its importance. The question arises that where does this alertness and awareness go, when the prestige of the nation comes on? If personal prestige, caste and community status, can be serious and the question of life and death, then why can't the same is applicable for the nation's reputation and interests?

Our personal reputation is hurt by a small incident and the prestige of the Indian nation is getting widespread for thousands of years, it is becoming dust-colored, his concern and any restlessness towards him does not compel us to take the path of struggle? Citizens are extremely alert and vigilant towards their personal dignity and respect, but this awareness becomes zero for the dignity and respect of the nation. As long as the eligible persons will not be indebted to important and decisive positions in India and an ideal governance-based system will not be built, India will remain in a state of inconvenience. Until qualified and meritorious person will not lead the country in all areas of life, by then the rise of the ultimate, prosperous and capable India will not be possible.

Creation of New India

If we are left behind in the form of a nation and society today and are unable to present any examples for the world, then we are really responsible for it. In the 21st century, this nation is re-emerging and giving us the opportunity to completely liberate the nation from the termite that has been found in the roots of the nation.

After all, how can we leave the tree under whose shadow we are sitting from generation to generations? Today, the nation needs to build a system of integrity and a true social system. For this, Indian citizens themselves have to adopt the path of integrity and patriotism. Only the change in power will not change the face of the nation. The political changes will not only liberate the nation. To determine this, the citizens of this nation have to prove their thinking, deeds, conduct and foresight.

Keep in mind that the conduct of each person is determined by the anticipation of the nation's future. Each moment every person of India is writing himself and the future of India by his actions. If our present is not more beautiful than its past, then it should also be a matter of serious contemplation for the present. No citizen can remain free from his responsibility and duties towards the nation. Every citizen of India has to self-analyze and evaluate. Only the elected government can create the future of the nation, but our conduct, personality and creativity, is being done as a nation by India or forming a nation every moment.

Due to the defect of individual worship today Nation-era is not anywhere in Indian politics. This situation must change immediately. This land, which is defamed by the politics, has to be reunited. Indian politics has been cursed by the worship of the person. Today, everywhere people will have to plant seeds of patriotism on the land of their minds. In Indian national life, every human being is born with the mother's womb as well as from the womb of another culture. The name of the same culture is Indianism.

It is clear that every Indian citizen has to understand and take responsibility for his motherland's birthplace. Unity, prosperity, climax and dignity of this Bharat land the obstacle needs to be destroyed in order to destroy each element. Glorious India be sure it must be the intended target of every Indian's life. In the absence of the national character, for thousands of years, we have seen this nation wandering in defeat, helplessness and slavery. In the absence of weapon and scripture, we are constantly being defeated. Our nationality and citizens have broken the spirit of worship of the nation. In fact, now we should have only one religion - 'Rashtra Dharma'. Now it is necessary that we should always think only and only about this nation. We sleep and wake up only for the concern of the nation.

Entangled in the diversity of beliefs, languages and sects, consciousness and sacrifices should not be given anymore. Keep in mind that the path of sect or faith can be different, but all of this will be ultimately the resource, not the goal. Actually life is a method, we all are followers. The one who is far superior to the truth, can't be ideal. There can't be any conflict between different religious systems, because ultimately the highest goal is 'Self-creation' and 'nation building'. Culture is, in fact, a tendency to have saturated life value and discipline in the daily life. It is necessary for us to rigorously evaluate and analyze our traditions and values in the light of truth.

It is absolutely certain that there is no other way left after leaving the path of truth. The downfall of a person, society and nation is always the only eternal reason - to be overturned by truth and justice. Only faith will not work in the values of truthful values. He has to take every citizen in his own conduct. For this, citizens will have to make their own example. Defective tendency, inferiority complex and somehow are engaged in selfishness by encouraging individuals, the nation can't be further strengthened. In the decades since the rise of this kind of political leadership, Indian politics and nation have collapsed. In fact, no person is important, but the nation itself is always important.

Creation of New India

The nation must be given the top priority. All of our other remaining responsibilities, such as parenting, living life, home-family, family-society, hobbies-entertainment, must be followed by it. If this sense and commitment to 125 crore Indian nation is ensured, then the great victory of this nation is sure. If this was possible, then in that very moment, we would be able to see that ultimate, glorious and capable India, taking place in front of us and taking a concrete shape. Today, the nation needs to be culturally, intellectually, socially and politically in one rope. Without this, the nation's cosmic will not be possible. The frustration and shortness spread all over the country and deep inside the citizens has to be eliminated from the root. Every citizen has to be animated with the national consciousness. Every Indian must be aware, alert and capable to discharge his duties and responsibilities towards the nation. Today, we need to create a national character. The creation of a national character is directly related to the character building of its citizens. The goal of complete change is also the person and the seeker is also the person. It is possible for a person to get a change from society and society to the nation. Politics can be made the way and center to bring about a universal change in life, because politics alone has the power to influence every area of life.

If politics will understand its responsibility for the nation and will consider the worship of this nation as the 'supreme religion', then it would be possible to restore the pride of the nation. When politics will ignore broad national interests, encourage the ineligible persons and will ignore anti-national elements and anti-national actions, so it has proved to be a destructive period for the nation.

It is clear that when the root of the tree is contaminated, how can the tree be free from disease? The 'nationalism' is to die for this nation and its protection. Every Indian should now worship, only this nation. Apart from this, no other superior or welfare way is no longer left, nor was it ever before, nor should it be. This is the right time when we have to build a healthy and new India without hypocrisy. This work has already been delayed, and further delay will be destructive.

NEW PUBLICATIONS

Biswaroop Roy Chowdhury
Dynamic Memory Computer
Course **(Updated & Revised)**

Dr. Ujjwal Patni
Power Thinking

Namita Jain
How to Lose the last
5 Kilos

Tarun Engineer
Aim High For Bigger Win

Joginder Singh
Mind Positive Life Positive

Yaggya Dutt Sharma
**The Lord of New Hopes
Akhilesh Yadav....**

Ashu Dutt
Master the Stock Market

Ashu Dutt
Stop Losing Start Winning

Renu Saran
101 Hit Films of Indian Cinema

Renu Saran
History of Indian Cinema

O.P. Jha
**Shirdi Sai Baba: Life Philosophy
and Devotion**

Dr. Sunil Vaid
Why Does My Child Misbehave

Biswaroop Roy Chowdhury
India Book of Records

Biswaroop Roy Chowdhury
Heal Without Pill

Surya Sinha
Perfect Mantras For Succeeding
in Network Marketing

OSHO
The Osho Upanishad

OSHO
Sermons in Stones

OSHO
Tantric Transformation

Subhash Lakhotia
Golden Key to Become
Super Rich

Subhash Lakhotia
Your Money My Advice

DIAMOND BOOKS X-30, Okhla Industrial Area, Phase-II New Delhi-110020
Tel : 0 11-40712200 email : sales@dpb.in

Shop online at www.diamondbook.in

9 789352 787715